ROBERT MCLEAN
JAMES A. DENSLEY

ROBBERY IN THE ILLEGAL DRUGS TRADE

Violence and Vengeance

BRISTOL
UNIVERSITY
PRESS

First published in Great Britain in 2022 by

Bristol University Press
University of Bristol
1–9 Old Park Hill
Bristol
BS2 8BB
UK
t: +44 (0)117 954 5940
e: bup-info@bristol.ac.uk

Details of international sales and distribution partners are available at
bristoluniversitypress.co.uk

British Library Cataloguing in Publication Data
A catalogue record for this book is available from the British Library

ISBN 978-1-5292-2391-0 hardcover
ISBN 978-1-5292-2392-7 ePub
ISBN 978-1-5292-2393-4 ePdf

The right of Robert McLean and James A. Densley to be identified as authors of
this work has been asserted by them in accordance with the Copyright, Designs
and Patents Act 1988.

Cover design: blu inc.
Front cover image: Rachel Bellinsky from stocksy.com

Contents

Notes on the Authors

Robert McLean, Ph.D., is Lecturer in the School of Education and Social Sciences at the University of the West of Scotland (UK).

James A. Densley, D.Phil. (Oxon), is Professor and Department Chair of Criminal Justice at Metropolitan State University (USA).

Acknowledgements

We wrote most of this book in 2020, which was a tough year to say the least. Before even the COVID-19 pandemic, my good friend Grant Henderson died in a car crash. Grant was a great guy who could light up any room. This book is yours, mate. You were, and still are, loved, and will be sorely missed.

I would also like to mention June, a great woman who always went above and beyond. Chris, I miss you too, mate. Fraser, Steve, Andy, and the rest, you will never be forgotten. Jack, I hope you are okay wherever you are.

On a separate, and lighter note, thanks to God for bringing into my life my loving wife Nicola and for blessing us with our beautiful children. What else could I ask for, honestly.

Robert McLean

Thanks to my family and friends for their love and support during a difficult year. I lost my dad in 2020 and it really put life in perspective. Andrew Densley served 25 years in the Leicestershire Police and was my entry point into the field of criminology. In ways large and small, he is the reason I write books like this. So, this one is for him. Thanks especially to my coauthor Robert for the opportunity to write it, and my wife Emily and children Alex and Andrew for the fun interruptions on cue that meant I kept coming back to it with fresh eyes and renewed energy.

James A. Densley

Acknowledgements

ONE

On Robbery

"Better make it £600, mate", Ricky instructs the young teller behind the counter at the Royal Bank of Scotland.

It's payday and Ricky can't wait to spend his earnings. Coloursfest, Glasgow's annual hard dance festival, is on the horizon, and thanks to an unusually hot summer, tickets are selling fast.

The rest of the lads already have theirs – Chewy, Big Del, Steggy Boy, even the Pollok lads. Early bird, half price. Ricky's paying full price though because last month his car broke down and fixing it took precedent. He can't afford being in overdraft. Again.

In truth, Ricky and the lads were too old for getting fucked up at a dance party.[1] Some of them had their own children now. But it was tradition, one night only to relive their glory days. Speaking of which, Ricky had enough cash on hand for a new set of sneaks and that Armani T-shirt he had had his eye on to compliment the Ralph Lauren shorts that were too big for his brother. Ricky wasn't just going to Braehead Arena, he'd be the best dressed there.

Ricky counts his cash again to make sure he hasn't been cheated. He never trusted bank tellers, or anyone really, and this kid looks barely old enough to count. Satisfied everything is kosher, Ricky walks out onto Renfrew High Street, 600 quid weighing heavily on his mind and in his pocket. It's a sunny Friday afternoon and the town is heaving. Ricky takes the back streets to avoid the crowds and cuts on to Houston, admiring the iconic red sandstone tenement block.

He calls his best friend Chewy on his mobile. Chewy answers immediately. He always does, it's like his phone is glued to his hand.

"All right, bud. Happenin', mate?" Ricky asks.

"Fuck all, ya dick," Chewy replies.

They insult each other for a minute. Glasgow lads do that.

"I'll just get you down in Braehead, mate. Outside Primark at the main doors round the back."

"Sound." Chewy hangs up.

Suddenly, someone calls out from the front steps of one of the three-storey tenement houses. An old drug addict begging for spare change. Ricky turns to the sound.

WHACK. Ricky's face meets a leaping punch from the top step. Everything goes black for a second, then warm.

Ricky's no stranger to a black eye and knows he's got another one coming. He quickly regains his senses and squares up to his assailant, who is tall, but rake thin, his body like so many around here, visibly ravished from years of heroin abuse.

A rush of adrenaline. "You fucking doing?" Ricky rages.

Ricky was a boxer in his youth. He sets himself to fight. But this won't be sporting. Ricky wants this to be ugly. A proper scheme booting,[2] no questions asked.

Surprisingly, the junkie stands his ground. Until—

A shooting pain in Ricky's back. A feeling from an old memory. A blade pressed hard against his left lung. Either a steak knife or a Kitchen Devils with fine serrations. The former is pretty common on the streets of Glasgow, used by posers trying to act tough. The latter is greater cause for concern. The weapon of choice for gang members at war or smackheads on the rob. Only those wanting to do you in right use a Kitchen Devils.

Ricky realized then he'd been done. Luckily, his thick Nike hoodie absorbed most of the knife's impact, but he could still feel a small trickle of blood running down his back. He was being robbed and not for the first time.

The first time was when he was 15. In a packed city centre in broad daylight, an older guy got away with two pounds after blindsiding Ricky and threatening to punch him "in the fucking face". Then, a few years later, at the bus stop after a night on the town, a couple of gang members pulled a Stanley utility knife on Ricky and his mate and demanded they both hand over their phones, jewellery, and cash. Ricky talked his way out of that one because the lads discovered they had mutual friends in common; his mate wasn't so lucky though, and still had his money and gold sovereign rings jacked.

This robbery was different. Ricky had fallen for the oldest trick in the book. One guy jumps out from an alley or side door to grab your attention, while the blade man sneaks up from behind and jams the knife hard against your back to immobilize you. Not a full stab, but just enough to pierce the skin and let you know they mean business.

A scrawny hand covered in home-made tattoos crawls over Ricky's shoulder. One of the tattoos reads 'REMO', or Renfrew Moorpark, a neighbourhood gang that used to run these streets back in the day.

"Don't fucking move or you're getting plugged, I fucking mean it," the tattoo guy says, close enough that Ricky can smell the cigarettes and alcohol on his breath.

"Gees the fucking money," the first guy says, agitated. He takes out a small lock-back knife and points it at Ricky's eye. He's not mucking about.

Ricky stands frozen. It's two versus one and he knows from the stories of his youth, at the height of the city's heroin epidemic, that you don't question whether or not drug addicts have the bottle to kill you when they are high or strung out and in need of a fix. Fear sets in and his legs turn to jelly.

"Right, here," Ricky says, defeated. He slowly removes his wallet from his pocket.

That should be the end of it, he thinks.

It's not.

WHACK. The guy in front clocks Ricky again, this time in the mouth. He's got that look in his eye. Black. Lifeless. Like a great white shark before a frenzied attack. Ricky knows if he doesn't act now, he's dead, or at least getting left for dead.

"Ya wee fucking prick," Ricky yells. He throws a wild, desperate right hook behind the left ear of his attacker. It rocks the man's equilibrium, who stumbles into the street, dropping the knife as he hits the ground amid some broken glass and smashed blocks of tar.

The tattoo guy grabs a handful of Ricky's hoodie. Ricky tries to wrestle free, pulling his arms and body through the sweatshirt in one swift motion – a move he perfected as a teenager when he got home past curfew and needed to get into bed quick before his mum walked in. But as he's doubled over, Ricky catches sight of that Kitchen Devils, the red handle rising quickly in an uppercut motion.

SWOOSH. The blade misses his face, but clips Ricky's left ear. It starts to bleed.

The tattoo guy is left holding the hoodie. A shirtless Ricky grabs him and pulls him into the thrust of a headbutt. Blood splatters as their faces collide with one another, nose to nose. The tattoo guy decks it and failing to break the fall with his arms, hits his head on the concrete.

Ricky, a bit dazed and confused, is the last man standing. He screams, blood all over his face, swiftly kicking the semi-conscious tattoo guy while he's down.

The first guy gets back on his feet, picks up the knife he dropped, and lunges at Ricky. Ricky backs up against the closed side gate of the tenement to find it's unlocked. He pushes through the threshold and out into the back courtyard, creating some much-needed distance.

"Get this cunt," the tattoo guy yells.

Ricky scans his surroundings for options. He tries the back gate. It's bolted shut. He thinks about jumping the fence. Seconds tick by. He waits. And waits.

Silence. No one is there.

Ricky walks back out onto Houston Street. His attackers have left without a trace. Left with Ricky's wallet and any aspirations he had for fun this summer.

"Fuck! For fuck's sake!" Ricky screams at the top of his lungs. An unhealthy mix of anger and humiliation setting in.

Suddenly a woman's voice breaks Ricky's reverie.

"You all right, son?" she asks. "That was fucking intense, eh?"

"Aye, misses, aye. It was, aye," Ricky replies.

"I seen it. I called the cops. They will be here soon," she says.

"You see what way they went?" Ricky asks, hoping not all is lost.

"You don't want to be going after them, do you? Nah, just wait on the polis."

"They have my wallet. I need it. Was 600 quid in it."

She points the way, without further hesitation. Like she knows that feeling of being six ton down.

"Thanks."

Ricky takes off. He calls Chewy for backup and he's en route, but it's a fruitless endeavour. The thieves are long gone.

Half an hour later, when the adrenaline rush wears off, Ricky remembers his abandoned hoodie. He doubles back to Houston Street.

The police are on the scene of the crime. Ricky shows up topless with a swollen eye, covered in blood.

"This yours?" one copper asks rhetorically, gesturing to Ricky's hoodie in his hand.

"Aye, it is."

"Can you tell me what happened here then?" the second officer asks, his tone suspicious and threatening.

"Aye, mate, I was jumped. Two junkies robbed me at knife-point and took 600 quid off me."

The officers are unconvinced. They blame Ricky for the robbery and accuse him of a drug deal gone bad. They chastise him for fighting back and chasing after the robbers. Things are tense. But before Ricky can speak his mind and make the situation worse, the woman who called the police in the first place intervenes and tells them Ricky is innocent. He's the victim. This time.

Putting this book (and robbery) in context

This is a book about robbery, specifically the lived experience of robbery from the perspective of victims and offenders. The narratives in this book capture the risks and rewards of a crime that can be planned or spontaneous. They capture the causes and consequences of robberies gone good and robberies gone bad, the adrenaline rush of the act, the at times precarious and explosive nature of the crime, and the gains and losses, both material and emotional.

Robbery attracts attention because it is both a violent crime and property crime, broadly defined as the act of taking or attempting to take anything of value by force, threat of force, or by putting the victim in fear (Smith, 2003). Indeed, under Scottish common law, robbery is theft brought about by violence or the threat of violence (the *actus reus*), wherein the offender intended to use violence or the threat of violence to acquire money or property (the *mens rea*) (McDiarmid, 2018). The term robbery conjures up the mythology of highwayman Dick Turpin and social bandits like Robin Hood, robbing from the rich and giving to the poor. Jesse James and his gang, robbing trains and banks. The Great Train Robbery, where in 1963, a gang of thieves escaped with £2.6 million from a Royal Mail train heading from Glasgow to London. *The Italian Job*, *Ocean's Eleven*, and other great Hollywood heists.

But the term robbery evokes more than just illegal entrepreneurship, that is, armed guys in ski masks knocking off jewellery stores and professional criminals living and dying by some sort of criminal code of honor (Hobbs, 1995). It also corresponds with the racialized moral panic around 'predatory' young Black males and 'mugging' (Hall et al, 1978). Fear of opportunistic 'economic-compulsive' crime (Goldstein, 1985) and amoral drug addicts in search of their next 'fix' or 'hit', robbing out of desperation. Finance capital robbing banks and banks robbing people's savings and loans so that corporate executives can profit (Black, 2014). In fiction and in fact, robbery takes many forms. Offenders can be young or old, rich or poor, and victims can be strangers or non-strangers.

For example, there is commercial robbery of banks, petrol stations, and convenience stores. 'Carjacking' and other vehicle-related robbery of armoured trucks and taxi drivers. Home invasions. Street robbery, meaning any offence that occurs in a public or semi-public place like a street, alleyway or park, including: purse-snatching; robbery at automated teller machines; robbery of drunken bar patrons; robbery of students on campus; and robbery of passengers on or near public transportation. A Home Office research study (Smith, 2003) identified five distinct types of street robbery: (1) blitz, the dramatic overwhelming of the victim to control or stun; (2) confrontation, that is, a demand for property using threats; (3) con, where victims are deceived into a form of street interaction; (4) snatch, where property is grabbed without any prior interaction; and (5) victim-initiated, meaning the victim initiates contact with the suspect such as via a drug deal or prostitution.

Robbery in any and all forms remains a comparatively under-researched crime in Britain. Most studies on robbery, especially those focused on offender decision-making and motivation, originate from the United States (for example Wright and Decker, 1997a). Drawing on interviews with 86 active armed robbers in St. Louis, Missouri, for example, Jacobs and Wright (1999) portray robbery as a *solution*. Offenders often are 'overwhelmed by their own predicament – emotional, financial, pharmacological and otherwise – and see robbery as the only way out' (1999, p 167). Shover (1996) observes similarly that individuals engaged in robbery tend to act under a sense of pressure, but any relief robbery provides is temporary. Decisions are made in the context of desperation, but also hedonism; with marginalized youth seeing robbery as the only viable means to achieve the sort of disposable income needed to support the conspicuous consumption that keeps them ahead of their peers in the competition for social esteem (Wright and Decker, 1997a).

Robbery in the US tends to be more lethal than in the UK, owing in large part to the wide availability of firearms (Zimring and Hawkins, 1999). Still, Wright et al (2006) suggest the motivations of UK street robbers match those of their American counterparts, and they must be understood within a cultural context where a reputation for toughness and destructive violence functions as capital and is highly prized. In such contexts, robbery may even exist as a form of 'street justice', combining reputation maintenance, loss recovery, and vengeance (Topalli et al, 2002; Jacobs and Wright, 2006).

Robbery offenders and victims tend to be men (Smith, 2003), and Deakin et al (2007) argue that older drug users are the most likely to use violence in the commission of robberies. Victim selection is predicated on 'a complex and insightful understanding of non-verbal communication and body language on the part of the offender' (2007, p 65), they argue, meaning violent victimization can be avoided through careful reading of behavioural cues and 'signals' (Densley, 2012), especially in spaces where the 'code of the street' thrives (Anderson, 1999). The notion of space is important to understanding the patterns of a predatory crime like robbery. Hallsworth's (2005) study of common street robbery, for example, draws on Routine Activities theory to explain why the crime converges around motivated offenders, suitable targets, and an absence of capable guardians (Cohen and Felson, 1979; Felson and Clarke, 1998). Related situational opportunity theories of crime have been central to how Britain has sought to reduce street robbery (for example Stockdale and Gresham, 1998; Tilley et al 2004).

This book focuses on robberies occurring in and around Scotland's *illegal drugs trade*, the sphere in which drugs are exchanged for money, goods, and services, where robbers and/

or their victims are drug dealers, drug users, or both (Marsh, 2019). It is important to note that this is a book about robbery first, not the function and structure of drug markets. Britain's illegal drugs market is complex (Pearson and Hobbs, 2001) and, thanks to globalization and technology, evolving (Densley et al, 2018; McLean et al, 2020; Whittaker et al, 2020). The market fluctuates, and as an end-user of drugs, Britain incorporates *importers*, suppliers who now live, or spend considerable time, overseas and arrange for drug shipments into the UK; *wholesalers*, who are typically UK-based organized criminals, who sell drugs in large quantities; and *retailers* who are the contact point for consumers (Pearson and Hobbs, 2001). Our focus here is when those importers, wholesalers, and retailers, including social suppliers and 'user-dealers' (Coomber, 2006), fall victim to robbery or use robbery as a tool or tactic. Think the notorious stick-up man Omar Little (Michael K. Williams) from HBO's *The Wire*, who made a career out of robbing street-level drug dealers.

Few studies directly and explicitly look at the role of robbery in the context of drug dealing. One exception is Jacobs' (2000) book, *Robbing Drug Dealers: Violence Beyond the Law*. Jacobs writes that in many ways, street-level drug dealers represent the 'perfect victim' because they are plentiful, visible, accessible, and they deal only in cash within a risky business where trust is hard-earned and easily lost. Drug deals provide the perfect set-up for a robbery because there is always money and drugs on scene, and when they are robbed in the course of doing business, drug dealers cannot call the police or file an insurance claim. Drug users find themselves in a similar predicament and the user/dealer nexus means lives often are precariously balanced. In their qualitative fieldwork with active offenders in St Louis, Jacobs and Wright (2008, p 511) found that robbery was at times more about 'sending a message' than generating capital. Market-related conflicts between trade partners and rivals were particularly common in and around urban drug networks, whereby the 'struggle for turf and market share' embroiled their participants in conflict that only violence could resolve (2008, p 515).

Another exception is Contreras' (2012) *The Stickup Kids*, which examines the inner workings of a group of Dominican drug robbers in the South Bronx who stalk and torture drug dealers storing large amounts of drugs and cash. The Stickup Kids share some similarities with the 'rip crews' documented by Gundur (2019) who attempt to steal wholesale stashes from drug smugglers between El Paso, Texas, US and Ciudad Juárez, Chihuahua, Mexico. Contreras (2012) documents in vivid detail how, after the crack cocaine economy went from boom in the 1980s to bust in the 1990s, crack dealers became violent drug robbers in an effort to salvage their lavish lifestyles. As amateur thieves become expert robbers, they are forced to self-medicate on marijuana and cocaine to cope with the excesses of expressive violence that turns brutal whenever victims refuse to cooperate.

Harding et al's (2019) typology of gang-related street robbery draws on some of the same fieldwork as this book. The authors found that gangs exist on a continuum, starting with recreational groups engaged in petty crime who align themselves to a set area of social space, such as a housing estate, park, or town centre, all the way up to more entrepreneurial and, eventually, organized crime groups (Densley, 2014; McLean, 2018). In recreational youth gangs, young men engaged in opportunistic robberies and expressive street violence to achieve masculine distinction. In criminal gangs higher up the food chain, robbing rival drug dealers was a means of 'gaining economic capital as opposed to symbolic capital' (Harding et al, 2019, p 892). And for organized crime gangs, robbery evolved to include fraud and money laundering, supplemented by (at times retaliatory) 'flash hold-ups' optimized to generate fear in rival gangs.

Robbery often occurs in the context of other crimes, and in the realm of drug crime it can have cascading consequences owing to 'the logic of violence' (Marsh, 2019). In Scotland, the 20-year blood feud between the Lyons and Daniels crime families, which culminated in numerous stabbings, shootings, and murders, was sparked by the robbery of a small quantity of drugs. The infamous Paisley Drugs Wars were similarly born out of crime families' attempts to govern Scotland's illicit drugs market, which included robbing drug dealers (see McLean and Densley, 2020). Attempts to avenge these robberies pulled other criminal actors and alliances into the ongoing feud. Once the fighting becomes endemic, however, many forget, or do not even know, what they are fighting about (Densley, 2013).

Data sources and methods

Drug dealers and users are an uncommon research sample owing to the illegality of their daily business. What sets this book apart is that it is shaped by the voices of actors who operate within illicit drugs markets, as opposed to those who seek to influence them externally, such as law enforcement. Influenced by 'narrative criminology' theory and mindful of the transformative power of stories that people tell about themselves in the world (Presser and Sandberg, 2015), this book captures the performative and contextual aspects of criminal behaviour in a way that is accessible to lay readers. Far too often, scholars claim to study crime, explain it, even predict it, without ever meeting or talking to a criminal. In so doing, they distance themselves from the people and lives they claim to be expert about, reducing real offending to ones and zeros on spreadsheets.

We break with this tradition, and like other urban ethnographers before us, lean into the people who feel they are misunderstood and misrepresented by wider society to ask them directly why and how they do what they do. This research is driven by a number of questions: What does robbery look and feel like? How does it come about? What roles are performed by the people involved? How are some targets selected and others dismissed? How do offenders weigh the morality of a crime like robbery? Do they enjoy frightening and harming others?

Does retaliation occur as a result? Was street justice present? Is there such a thing as a criminal code? What are the outcomes? Why do offenders continue to rob when all evidence and experience points to a negative return on investment? What role does law enforcement play? How, if at all, does robbery affect the community and wider public?

This book offers a reinvigorated and contemporary understanding of a life in crime, anchored in the 'neglected' perspective of serious violent offenders (Wright and Bennett, 1990, p 138). It embraces the fact that crime is complex, contextual, personal, and is shaped by the wider socio-cultural and political climate. It is built on eight years (from 2012 to 2020) of ethnographic fieldwork in Glasgow and West Scotland and qualitative interviews with a snowball sample of 75 men and eight women aged 16–60 who were at one time involved in or affected by gang and group offending and/or activity defined by Police Scotland as 'organised crime' (for a discussion, see McLean, 2019). They were accessed initially via social service providers and faith-based organizations, who acted as gatekeepers. Five practitioners and eight local community residents also were interviewed to help validate and triangulate information.

Additional interviews were conducted with 38 active young street offenders who were accessed via 21 practitioner-interviewees working in youth crime prevention and intervention services (for a discussion, see Deuchar et al, 2022). Bar a few phone and FaceTime interviews and a couple of group interviews, all interviews were conducted one-on-one, face-to-face, and lasted anywhere from 30 minutes to five hours (with one hour being the average). Interviews were either digitally recorded and selectively transcribed or captured directly via voice notes. The data were coded and analyzed thematically – only the themes pertinent to robbery feature in this book. Verbatim quotes (with the distinctive Glaswegian slang and patois fully preserved) are used throughout the book to illustrate these themes. Pseudonyms are used to preserve the confidentiality of the respondents, and some details have been spliced and edited for the same reason.

The University of the West of Scotland granted ethical approval for the study. Participation was voluntary and predicated on the active and informed consent of all research participants. Standard ethical principles were followed regarding informed consent, right to withdrawal, and data protection. The first author tapped into his own social network and leveraged his own personal history as a crime victim and offender, to access some interviewees (see McLean and Densley, 2020). For example, it was Robert's cousin who first introduced him to Kevin, a handsome, soft-spoken young man – over 20 years ago.

"You fae here, mate," uttered Kevin with a hint of scepticism. This was the usual line of questioning when new people met outside of their home area.

"Aye, mate, stay in [town], moved here a few months ago," Robert explained.

"Not seen you at school. You a Tim?" making reference to the fact Robert did not attend the local non-denominational school with Kevin, and in a city divided by religious sectarianism, the only other option was for Robert to be Catholic (a 'Tim Malloy') and attend Catholic school.

"Nah, mate." Robert laughed, lifting his tracksuit top to show a Glasgow Rangers football shirt underneath. Traditionally, Rangers supporters are Protestant while Celtic fans are Catholic.

Kevin was a Rangers fan too. And from this briefest of interactions, Robert and Kevin became firm friends, united by a keen interest in football, amateur boxing, and girls.

At age 16, Robert left school and started working, first as labourer, then in a call centre, and later in a garage. Kevin was a year younger and still stuck at school, so Robert saw him less and really only on weekends or occasionally at the boxing gym. It was there Robert first noticed a change in Kevin, namely a dip in form. Kevin was training less and getting sloppy in the ring. He was drinking and socializing more, so much so that Kevin had been spotted unconscious, lying on the street or in a bush. After carrying a drunken Kevin home one night, Robert tried to warn him about the dangers of excess drinking, but avoided a proper intervention because it was deemed unmanly by local, working-class, standards. He regrets that now because Kevin was clearly drinking himself into oblivion and it wasn't long before his drink problem evolved into a drug problem.

To feed his habit, Kevin started robbing local youth on the street. He later robbed a mutual friend, Sean. Sean was a petty drug dealer sourced by an older cousin, and a bit of a "punk". Kevin said as much one night at a party, adding Sean was a "loud mouth" in need of a "serious slap". The robbery, however, took everyone by surprise. An intoxicated Kevin held Sean against his will for some time before taking his money, some items of jewellery and clothing, and his drugs. This caused a rift in the group and Robert then stopped hanging out with Kevin.

About a year later, Robert was walking home one night and spotted Kevin on the street. Kevin was too drunk to stand straight and lunged at Robert, apparently trying to rob him. Kevin fell flat on his face on the concrete. When Robert next saw him, sober, Kevin had no recollection of the event. That was the last time they saw each other for some time, although Robert heard rumours that Kevin stabbed a guy on the street and later a shopkeeper in another botched robbery and he eventually ended up in prison.

Fast-forward nearly two decades, and Robert is a criminologist studying robbery. He coincidentally bumps into Kevin, who upon learning about Robert's career and research agenda, agreed to sit for an interview. Robert asked him about that night with Sean. Kevin said it had been driven by a combination of jealously, alcohol, and drug addiction, which brought out negative emotions and poor decision-making. He was clean now and expressed remorse for his actions, even admitting that after getting out of prison he tried to make amends by paying back some of the money. Although Kevin added he still wanted to give Sean a firm backhand across the face to "wipe the smirk off".

The interview had been cathartic for Kevin, part of his own recovery process, a 'redemption narrative' of sorts (McAdams, 1997; Maruna, 2001). So, Robert decided to reach out to Sean via social media to get his side of the story. In a subsequent interview, Sean talked about having 'nightmares' about his encounter with Kevin, not so much from the physical attack, but rather from feeling emasculated and humiliated. He said the robbery taught him a valuable lesson about the dangers of 'going solo' in the drugs game (Windle and Briggs, 2015) and from that point on he carried a weapon everywhere he went and he sought out partners in crime who had better 'criminal credentials' than him (Gambetta, 2009, p 3). Sean then disclosed that he had recently served time in prison himself for stabbing a would-be attacker. It was clear that his experience as a robbery victim had fundamentally changed his life's trajectory.

This vignette highlights the purposive sampling and personal connections that lie at the heart of primary research with hard-to-reach populations. There are pros and cons to leveraging one's 'status as an insider' (Hobbs, 1988, p 15) because shared history can introduce (conscious and unconscious) forms of bias. But in the end, it allowed us to see both sides of this robbery offence (victim and offender), challenge conventional wisdom that 'friends don't rob friends' (Jacobs, 2000, p 56), and understand the decades-long consequences when they do. Throughout this book, in cases where both victim and offender(s) have been interviewed, we endeavour to examine both sides of the story.

In some cases, interviewees sat for multiple follow-up interviews about 'life and crime in Glasgow' (McLean and Densley, 2020). Glasgow is the largest city in Scotland, but not its capital, and for decades it was regarded as a redundant, post-industrial 'city of gangs', divided by sectarianism and fuelled by alcohol and violence (Deuchar, 2009; Davies, 2013; Fraser, 2015). The Scottish Index of Multiple Deprivation has consistently shown that a disproportionate number of the country's most deprived communities are located in and around

Glasgow (Scottish Government, 2020). Poverty and inequality are entrenched, with over a fifth of the city's children living in unemployed households, and in some communities, over 50 per cent of youth live below the poverty line (Glasgow Indicators Project, 2015). Since the 1980s, cheap, high potency, brown, smokable heroin has become a dangerous adaptation to poverty and deprivation in Glasgow, spawning an entire '"Trainspotting" generation' of drug addicts (Daly, 2017). Indeed, 'levels of problematic drug use … and drugs crime [in Scotland] are among the highest in the world' (McCarron, 2014, p 17). There are approximately 50,000 heroin users in Scotland (Casey et al, 2009), and drug addiction has become both a way of life and a leading cause of Scotland's high mortality (Walsh et al, 2017).

This explains in part our research emphasis on robbery in the context of Scotland's illegal drugs trade (McLean et al, 2018). Robbery became a central theme after we began probing around issues of trust in illicit drug markets and the precautions our interviewees took to avoid detection, not just from law enforcement, but also from other criminals. It appeared to us that drug dealers feared other drug dealers more than they feared the police, in part because so many of them had been burned in the past by their own partners in crime. Theft, double-dealing, "grassing" – and robbery – were rife among the criminal fraternity, they said. Further, drug dealers, particularly at the retail level, appeared to think nothing of ripping off their own customers, which seemed counter-intuitive to building a sustainable business, even an extra-legal one.

This book demonstrates that among the criminal fraternity in Glasgow and West Scotland, robbery is endemic, a perennial threat for young men living in what Hallsworth (2013) describes as 'violent street worlds'. The data show robbery has become more common but less sophisticated over time, as is characterized now by limited planning, practice, and prowess. The rewards of robbery have steadily declined, moreover, yet the risks and harms – specifically, violent victimization – have significantly increased. As Ricky's story at the start of this chapter shows, what separates a robbery from a murder is at times just a matter of luck and inches.

For offenders, robbery achieves an instrumental goal of economic gain, but also an expressive goal of masculine status- and thrill-seeking. For victims, robbery involves the loss of money or possessions, but also a lingering sense of humiliation and emasculation. Victims often are left pondering whether what they did contributed at all to their own victimization or renders them vulnerable to revictimization. This is especially true when robbery is performed with or in front of peers and actions or reactions fail to live up to expectations.

Looking ahead

This book offers new empirical insights into the crime of robbery. It is divided into seven chapters. This first chapter opened with a narrative account of robbery drawn from our ethnographic fieldwork with active offenders in Glasgow and West Scotland. It then outlined the book's purpose, its contribution, methodology, and structure; it has also situated the current study within the existing literature and the research site. We observe how, in academic criminology, there has been a gradual shift away from looking at the life worlds of those who actually commit crimes and how this book is intended to return to exploring the lives and crimes of our interviewees in detail.

Chapter Two examines the evolution of robbery, namely how globalized changes have widened and somewhat diluted the crime. Here we explore why offenders choose robbery in general over other crimes (for example burglary, shoplifting) and robbing drug dealers specifically over commercial forms of robbery. This chapter also covers the dynamics of competition at different tiers of the illicit drugs market.

This leads into Chapter Three on the will to rob. What motivates robbery in illicit drugs markets? A number of issues are explored, such as monetary rewards, drug use and addiction as stimulants for robbery, drug debts and debt-bondage, and personal, emotional drivers.

Chapter Four documents the practice of robbery, mostly at the lower end of the drug market where younger social suppliers, retail-level dealers, petty criminals, end-users, and drug addicts converge. It explores how targets are selected, how information is gathered on selected targets, how stash houses are infiltrated, the precautions taken to avoid robbery, and retaliation (or not).

Chapter Five demonstrates there is no honour among thieves with examples of intra-gang robberies, getting set up, and criminals putting friends and enemies out of business.

Chapter Six examines life after robbery, with the conclusion of Ricky's robbery ordeal from Chapter One and a discussion of the process of desistance from robbery careers. This chapter emphasizes religion as both a method and motive for criminal desistance.

The final chapter discusses the findings from the book and situates them within the wider theory and research on robbery. Some limitations and then implications for future research and practice are discussed.

TWO

From Robbing Places to Robbing People

Glasgow and West Scotland's career criminals have long been implicated in predatory crimes such as robbery, theft, and burglary. Reminiscing about his early years in law enforcement, former police officer David said: "Old time [criminals] carried out robbery. [Of] course, banks getting robbed. More, before I really started [or] joined the force. [Hold-ups] when wages were getting delivered to works was common." However, countless (auto)biographical accounts written by, for, or about local hardmen and 'gangsters' describe a shift in emphasis in the criminal underworld in recent decades (see Boyle, 1977; Ferris, 2005; Findlay, 2012; Johnson, 2017), whereby robbers gradually turned their attention away from robbing *places* (for example banks, post offices, and jewellery stores) to robbing *people*, specifically fellow offenders.

This change began with the implementation of 'situational crime prevention' measures in Britain in the 1970s (Felson and Clarke, 1998; Clarke, 2012). Target hardening techniques and technological innovations like closed-circuit television (CCTV) and time-delay locks made robbing banks infinitely more difficult (Pitts, 2008). Goldsmith, a convicted armed robber, long retired, told us, "It is harder to do a bank over. It can be done, but not in the same way as once before. You see the Hatton crew [a reference to the 2015 Hatton Garden underground safe deposit burglary] … it is more theft."

Criminals needed a new venture, Goldsmith explained, and in the 1980s a new supply route linking Afghanistan to Iran presented an opportunity. Afghani and Pakistani heroin that flowed through Europe suddenly became more available, and affordable. This sudden supply glut saw heroin prices drop in Scotland and drug addiction boom. Drugs are an inelastic product, meaning (a) demand remains unchanged even when the price changes, and (b) criminals can make big money servicing an addicted clientele. The drugs 'business' quickly became more predictable and profitable than the ad hoc 'blags' of a yesterday (Hobbs, 1988; Pitts, 2008; see also, O'Mahoney and Ellis, 2009).

Gone were the days of a getaway car, shotguns, and a crew, Goldsmith explained, and with them went the 'criminal code':

G: Every fucking bastard out there shifting a sniff of gear [drugs] now believes he is a ticket [gangster] ... Dealers will sell to kids. Wreck communities. No [morals], no, nothing. [Older professional criminals] got respect. Stole from the wealthy. No[t] the poor.

Interviewer: *I see what you're saying.*

G: It is about money. It has always been about money. That is why I [committed armed robbery]. But it was not the same. The rush from pulling up in the car, brimmed and loaded. It cannot be outdone. The money and [the thrill] went [hand in hand] ... I get it man, I honestly get it. I see why punters will move [to selling drugs]. I couldn't. Just couldn't.

I: *Was it not something that you ever considered, having always been involved in like crime?*

G: No. I wasn't going to get a fucking job either. No[t] at my age now ... [Drug

> dealers] are bullies, a fucking virus on the
> planet. I have no respect for them. They
> are not criminals, fucking vermin. I can
> see why it might be justification to take
> money from them. The thought crossed
> my mind, course … [but] end of it all, it
> is still drug money. Tainted, isn't it not?

Goldsmith witnessed first-hand the 'turns' in the criminal underworld where robbery became more difficult and simultaneously less profitable and former colleagues turned to drug distribution in an effort to maintain the 'fast money' lifestyle they were accustomed to. Career criminals essentially had a choice to make: move with the times or be rendered obsolete, and in many cases, their existing 'criminal capital' (McCarthy and Hagan, 1995; 2001) made the transition seamless.

Goldsmith frowned upon his colleagues that went 'the easy route' into drugs, but he noted a more palatable (for him) middle ground wherein the old commercial robbers refocused their efforts on robbing different, easier, targets – drug dealers. Drug dealers had no recourse to the law and could hardly complain if they were robbed by other criminals, said Goldsmith; that's the price you pay for playing a dirty game.

A number of our interviewees discussed "abducting", "capturing", or "snatching" drug dealers and holding them against their will on behalf of organized criminals. Jack told us the con involved getting victims' family members and close friends to pay a ransom that would be used to clear any outstanding drug debts:

> 'Snatched the daftie right off the street … in pure
> daylight, mate … [of course] it was dodgy but the
> arsehole is a pure rat man … was in 10G [£10,000]
> … need to grab him or he would have been off …
> vanished … put it this way, after spending a few days in
> our company, he paid up … well, no' him directly …

say he was kind of incapacitated [laughs] ... few phone calls and you would be surprised how quick people get the money together for these scumbags ... if your son's a junkie, he's a fucking junkie ... wouldn't be me paying for them if it was my boy.'

Jack and his friend actually received a custodial sentence for their part in this crime and others involving the same victim and his family, but Jack and other participants in the study indicated that many similar events go unreported because drug dealers are 'fair game'.

When asked about the morality of robbing drug dealers, another interviewee, Hugh, sounded a lot like Goldsmith:

'Robbing drug dealers? Fuck off. It is doing the community a service, no? Aye, sure it is, am saying it. I don't pollute the place wi' that pish. Fucking use it [the money] to get the things we need. Give it to my mates, what have you, you know, whoever needs it.'

Hugh saw nothing wrong in taking money from drug dealers and spending it on himself and his loved ones. He blamed the victims, a common 'technique of neutralization' (Sykes and Matza, 1957), to justify his actions. Robbing drug dealers weighed little on his conscience because drug dealers deserved to be robbed – they were "vermin", people who plagued the community, Hugh said. They were less than human. And by robbing drug addicts too, Hugh unfairly saw himself as "helping" them:

'[The way] I see it, I'm doing them a favour, aren't I? The guy's only going to go and spend his hard-earned money on crap, make himself a pure, fucking flopping about the place, idiot on the stuff. Better in my [pocket] than his own if he is going to be an idiot wi' it. Am I no right, eh?'

Working for the man

David policed organized drug crime for years. He argued that at first, "drugs were not high on the agenda" because they "were not popular", especially "harder drugs". Drug use was really only associated with minor offending such as petty theft, shop lifting, and general anti-social behaviour. His weekends were spent largely "patrolling the [town centre] for closing time, pubs closing for the night. Dealing with drunks, getting everybody up the road safely". But then, "by 1988, 1989, maybe 1990, that is when I really noticed the real trouble with drugs … Heroin brings trouble. We had a high number of assaults, stabbing, battery, [linked] to [a] feud between dealers". David recalled one case where a drug dealer kidnapped a rival dealer then "was shot right through the eye in a busy pub" in retaliation. Another dealer "was also shot. In the legs, I am sure", then "a car got shot up right outside the front of the court as well", all within a matter of weeks. He went on:

> 'That gave us a real incentive, maybe an eye-opener, to the real issue, of hard drugs … [Prior to this] I think, most thought drug users were a nuisance, low-level [petty criminals] … Cause trouble, but were nothing more. [The aforementioned incidents] were, as I said, an eye-opener that the real guys, the top end players, had now seen the luxuries [selling] drugs brought, [not robbing] shops, post offices, your groceries, and what sorts. I knew after then drugs were going to be where the future of policing serious, organized criminality would go.'

As overdoses and heroin-related deaths in Scotland increased dramatically, police prioritized drug crime, often through a public health lens because needle-sharing was implicated in the rise of other fatal diseases, HIV and AIDS. Police also observed an increase in the use of recreational drugs among young people, first of all cannabis (Parker et al, 1998), then the new 'dance drugs' like ecstasy (Windle, 2013). But their biggest concern was Scotland's career criminals turning away from predatory-based organized crime, namely commercial robbery, and leaning into market-based organized crime, especially the drugs trade and related mafia 'governance' crimes like racketeering and extra-legal protection (von Lampe, 2016).

For example, one of the most recognizable criminal figures in Scotland, Paul Ferris (2005), notes that in this context he was recruited to serve as an enforcer for drug kingpin, and Glasgow's godfather, Arthur Thompson Senior. Ferris had been an armed robber in a series of jewel heists and Thompson was an experienced safecracker before making the switch to drug supply. Infamous debt collector Shaun Smith and enforcer Stephen French (Johnson, 2017) likewise used their martial arts, street fighting, and weightlifting skills to (literally) muscle in on local drug dealers who came to their attention. French was even nicknamed 'The Devil' because he kidnapped and tortured the drug dealers he robbed (Johnson, 2017).

Robbery didn't disappear from the crime landscape, therefore, it simply evolved to become part of the illegal drugs trade. Darren, who is well known in the criminal fraternity as a fence who buys and sells stolen goods, observed: "Folk are robbing folk all the time. There isn't no way of getting away from it. [Individuals] have to always be watch[ing] their back[s]. Folk I know who have done the dirty on their mates for a couple of grams is bang out now."

A number of our interviewees had made robbing drug dealers their specialty. Often this meant being involved in drug dealing themselves, but mostly to offload what they robbed. To be specialized in this arena, robbers required a number of resources including access to firearms, stolen vehicles, and information; the latter of which was key. Following a tip that a local drug dealer had a high four-figure sum in his house, and some jewellery, for example, career criminal Earl was encouraged to take action:

'Soon as I got wind, I got in touch with [David]. He is [legit]. Got in his van and got in touch with my boy to get on ready to move [the anticipated stolen jewellery], we were on the move. David was going to break the lock. Easy as that. In with [our contact], as he knew where it was. Said in the kitchen, but am no' ripping the place [apart]. In and out.'

Often this information came from serious organized criminals involved in drug distribution who use robbery to secure supply chains, limit the social mobility of others, or eliminate the competition entirely. For a cut of the profits, such individuals may also provide the resources necessary for colleagues to partake in robbery as a steady business venture, including access to firearms and other criminal commodities or legitimate contacts, such as people who could help move stolen goods or launder the proceeds of crime.

In the 1992 Quentin Tarantino film, *Reservoir Dogs*, the main antagonist who organized the diamond heist was a character named Joe Cabot, played by Lawrence Tierney. Joe was a crime boss who specialized in armed robberies, hijackings, and moving and selling stolen property. Joe put together 'jobs', along with his son 'Nice Guy' Eddie Cabot, by recruiting different career criminals and planning out the details of each robbery. In the course of our research, we learned about people like Joe in real life, who would connect one criminal with another in order to carry out a particular robbery job or related debt collection:

'I didn't know [him] before from like before getting involved with [OC group]. [OC group member A] said, "Here is [Jimmy]. Go with Jimmy and he will show you where you have to go. Be nice to each other." That was how I met him … [we] only [worked] together two times.' (William)

'I didn't know the guy personal. My mate [approached me] and asked if I would collect some money for his mum's pal, maybe his aunt's mate, can't remember exactly … I thought it would be the usual, until I got to the house. Belter of a house up the Mearns. Chapped the door and a pure gimp [weak] cunt answers, asked if he was [name] … [and] gave the cunt the whole spiel: "You know who I am?", "You know who I run wi'?", that shit. Obviously, the cunt had no idea who I was, think he was a doctor or something, [so] why the fuck would he know who I am [laughs] … Soon clicked after I lifted my top and showed a shooter [gun], fake, mind you, but he didn't know that … the posh cunt gives over about £3,000 … I have to actually drive him to his fucking dad's house to help him get it. Fucking sitting in his dad's house, living room, while he is making me fucking tea [laughs] … turns out it was [a professional] that had been owed money for letting an apartment [to the debtor]. Only found out cause my mate was out of town and had me drop it right to his house. Wouldn't believe the cunts, fucking meant to be squeaky clean as well … [who would be] asking you to get their money.' (Reese)

On one occasion, Reese was even hired to snatch someone's pet as collateral. He said: "No joke … [We had to] collect a fucking dog, a wee Akita pup … [from] her ex-boyfriend."

A good name and reputation or 'rep' in the criminal underworld was what afforded these interviewees the opportunity to work for more serious organized criminals (for example, see Rahman et al, 2020). In many cases, reputations had been built from a young age to be cashed in and rewarded with other criminal opportunities. Some opportunities paid well but involved significant risk. Alan told us:

'[When] we done [robbed] [OC group A's drug] stash over at the flats in town, we got about a kilo in Chico [ready cut cocaine], I would say so. Aye, think about that. Probably just over to be honest, cause some was already bagged to go ... I got about eight G [£8,000] for that hit. Same wi' the [other gang members], more or less, aye. It was worth more but we had to punt it on fast ... I kept the weed I took, wee [gang member A] took the speed we got off [victim A] ... think there was around £13,000. That went to [OC group B] ... [because] that's [gang member A's] brother, well, step-brother [a member of OC group B]. Was him that tipped us off.'

Alan explained that the armed robbers were hired by an established organized crime (OC) group. The group worked more in market-based OC, thus only ever wanted to be involved with predatory crimes like robbery "at arm's length". Acting as informational middlemen afforded them plausible deniability and some insulation from any blowback. Mafioso similarly operate in that 'middle man' niche (Reuter, 1983), leveraging their criminal reputations to enforce their will and govern underworld transactions. Another interviewee, Ewan, observed:

'We take nothing to do with [it] ... like, say, I don't know, Mr Jones, [but Mr Jones has, say, £10,000 worth of E's [ecstasy], I would [say], "Hold on, mate, I know a guy that might be interested" and then phone [Mr Smith], cause that's his field man, he deals with that ... Course I take a cut but for doing that, don't work for fuck all ... and basically making sure [Mr Jones] doesn't get bumped.'

Ewan's group focused only on one or two specific illegal goods, which allowed them to operate more efficiently and retain a clear trail of thought and action. Diversification resulted in "getting sloppy and fucking up". The fact that Ewan stated, "I take a cut", as opposed to 'we take a cut', indicated that while Ewan drew upon his group's reputation in his business, he exploited this reputation to earn profit for himself, which is something well documented in studies of mafia groups (for example Gambetta, 1993). Ewan demonstrates that as part of a well-established OC group, he was able to exert power and control over others, using hard-earned criminal capital to do so; thus, he can take a cut of the profits and tax others wishing to participate in his criminal network.

Adapting to change: starting a robbery career

Socko, Fraser, and Christopher grew up together in a large town within the greater Glasgow conurbation. Christopher was local, but Socko moved there from the South Side of Glasgow and Fraser from the East End, and they brought with them criminal connections tied to family and friends in the city:

> **F**: I was born in Glasgow, not Paisley … [I must] have been about 12, might have been 13 before my mum moved [to the town]. [Be]cause I was starting secondary … So aye, S1 [year one]. Socko came into my school not long before we were leaving.
>
> **S**: Aye, I knew Fraser from maths and English classes.
>
> **F**: I met Christopher cause [the local youth] football team.
>
> **S**: Same, mate.

Socko and Fraser had prolific criminal histories and offended well into early adulthood. Socko even spent time behind bars for robbery, weapon carrying, and drug supply. Our interviews with the three friends together captured general changing attitudes toward robbery tied to the growth of the illegal drugs trade throughout the 1990s and into the 2000s. They began by describing their offending as adolescents, including fighting and anti-social behaviour, but also an early flirtation with robbery:

> **S**: Me and Fraser did [socialize] a fair bit. Like my mates were mates with his mates and we knew each other from school.

F: And footy.

C: All the guys in the schemes got on well enough. We would hang out on the Friday and Saturday nights getting pissed [drunk].

I: *Would fights break out when you were all drinking? Like scheme rivalry, and all that?*

C: Aye, it could happen.

F: Could say that.

S: Aye, but no like all the time.

C: A fair bit with like one-on-one fights and that. No like pure gang scrapping.

F: Aye. We [all] went to school together so people spoke, but fights can kick off when drink is involved.

S: An uneasy truce you could say [laughs]…

F: Most the shit that we were into, was like, what most wee guys do – scrapping, panning windows, attacking buses.

C: Stealing cars as well.

F: Aye, that's good. Mind, Steve dropped that car off at the pitch [laughing].

C: Comes back and it is all smashed to fuck [laughing]…

I: *What about other things, like crime for money?*

F: Like stealing or robbery?

I: *Aye, stealing, theft, robbery, that sort?*

F: No like a pure thing.

S: Suppose, at 14 you're no' thinking 'bout making money. Most the shit is about having a laugh and being full of the bravado.

F: I would think it was more around 16 that we would be hearing of mates robbing folk.

S: Aye, it was 16 that I did my first robbery.

Sixteen was a critical age for these young men because it was then that they realized aggression, bravado, and risk-taking could only take them so far. At 16, young people need money; money to consume the goods and services, like high-end designer clothing and trips to the pub, that make them attractive to the opposite sex. A quick way to make money was low-level drug dealing, and an even quicker route to riches was theft, but stealing brought negative connotations, so individuals were reluctant to engage:

> **F**: I have to say I was never into stealing stuff.
>
> **S**: I know. I would steal drink from [the local superstore] but that was all. If you are stealing you get a name for being a thief.
>
> **F**: Not a good look, you know.
>
> **S**: Defo, mate. I jacked it in [gave up] cause I remember wee Ryan had a house party and didn't let me in. Was a heavy rid neck. I know it was cause the stealing. He told James that was why I couldn't get in. [In] case I bump his stuff. I stole from [the superstore] but would never do that from a mate's house. Low, low.
>
> **F**: Aye, it gives that perception. People see you as untrustworthy.

Being labelled a thief was not a good look, Socko and Fraser agreed. Other interviewees in the study felt the same. Occasionally, people would sell stolen goods like clothing and electronics in closed networks to peers or in open networks in local pubs and recreational clubs to make some additional money, but even lifting some alcohol on a Friday night from a large "faceless" supermarket, when you lacked the funds to buy it, could potentially ruin your reputation as someone to be trusted.

Street robbery was something qualitatively different in the minds of our interviewees. Not only was it the fastest way for a young lad to make money, its relationship with violence elevated the crime in the eyes of others:

> **I**: *What was [the first robbery at 16] like?*
>
> **S**: Me, aye?

I: *Yeah. If you don't mind?*

S: It's sound. Aye. I just needed cash, like I don't really know why I did it. Looking back, I would say it was just like stress for cash to actually live. But, it could be like a natural movement that people do when they come from the kind of background I come from … [a known] criminal [family].

I: *Were you scared?*

S: Fuck, why would I be scared? I had the knife. The other boy didn't.

I: *Well, more nervous?*

S: See, you're right. Actual. I was scared. I would be lying. I was scared, like a nervousness. It doesn't seem real. Like in the moment, it just don't feel it is happening. I was scared just for a wee second when I opened my mouth. But soon as I said 'mate', to call him over, fear went, and it was just like I was [a] robot, saying a set script.

Socko stated that while robbery initially was born from feelings of stress for money, in much the same way that cannabis is seen as a gateway drug to harder drugs down the line, his family reputation and prior recreational delinquency was a route to more serious, profit-oriented crime later in life.

Fraser reported he committed his first robbery at age 17, but he had been a victim of robbery many times before that in his early teens. His experience as a victim was actually something that contributed to Fraser becoming an offender:

F: I had been robbed a few times when I was younger. Just like in the town. Older guys, gangs or junkies and mad chancers trying to take money off me, and my mates … I do think that now I am older and think back, that these things traumatized me a bit. I would be scared when I thought of being robbed but you're young and palm it off as 'shit happens'.

> Wasn't long after I got battered and robbed, and my trainers stolen and jacket as well. Not long after that, that kind of time period, I would start carrying [a knife] … I used that knife in a robbery me and Chris did. In town, just no reason, I pulled the blade and robbed these three wee guys.
>
> **C:** They were our age, but maybe a year or two younger.
>
> **F:** Aye. I am almost a full year older than you no[w].

Prior research has found that youth in Glasgow carry weapons in public for protection and in response to news about local crime, and experiences of victimization, both real and perceived (Holligan et al, 2017). Likewise, Fraser's actions show that prior victimization set him up psychologically, but also practically (in terms of carrying a knife for protection) to partake in robbery. In some ways, robbing others became his way of coping and owning the fact that he had been robbed himself. Chris notes that around that same time, inspired by Fraser's actions, a few local delinquent youths also began robbing people:

> **C:** We weren't the only boys. It was as though all our mates started doing it. It became like a thing, you know what I saying?
>
> **F:** Like we started a trend.
>
> **C:** Aye.
>
> **F:** Even people we didn't know, know, but knew of from other schools, were doing more robberies.

Yet these poorly planned and often poorly executed robberies came with repercussions, including police attention and criminal justice consequences, to the extent that the risks started to outweigh the rewards. This resulted in the lads thinking more strategically about target selection:

> **S:** I [was] charged with a robbery. It was dropped. Then Shuggie was jailed. A heavy sentence as well after he

robbed the local garage. He ran in and just held it up with only his fists. His first mistake. A heavy, known woman, an older woman … worked the night shift. She is solid and…

C: Aye, sure she was, [she was] one of the suspects in the shooting in town!

I: *What happened to him?*

S: Aye, she whipped out a bat, smacked him over the back, and literally chased him right down [the main] road. He got three years inside for that and literally left the place with fuck all.

Such stories of failure were not uncommon. Arguably more so because of the immaturity and inexperience of teens who were engaging in violent crime for profit for the first time. Socko recalled another similar incident:

S: Big Clive as well. He got three years for robbing a post office. Was the one right round the corner from the place Shuggie robbed. About the same time as well. So was doomed to fail, with everyone getting their cameras up and working and more police about … he got into the back of the post office and grabbed money from the wee worker … Snatched it and made off. But she went to our school, [so she recognized him] and told the police who it was. See when they went to his house, the fucking daft idiot had the exact money to the pence in his bedroom drawer. Who would even do that? You would break it up.

C: Fuck knows why he stole the change as well [laughs].

With long prison terms for those who were trying to learn the trade, it was found that other targets made much easier pickings and brought less reprisals as well. With the booming drugs trade, and the relatively young age of the youths who were either using or dealing drugs at the time, robbery within the illicit drugs market became the solution. Drug dealing was illegal and disputes could not be settled by police, which made dealers (a) responsible for their own protection and (b) vulnerable if they were ever caught lacking. Contreras (2012), Jacobs (2000), and others have all found that robbing drug dealers is popular among offenders because their engagement in criminality means they rarely have recourse to the law.

After his friend Shuggie went to prison, Socko changed his tactics and starting robbing drug dealers; at first, newcomers at the lower end of the scale. "They knew what they were getting into" was how Socko justified his actions. Peer-on-peer robbery was an expected, or at least well understood, part of 'The Game' (Harding, 2014) and within the rules of the game, 'snitching' or reporting to the police is unlikely owing to the illegality of drug dealing (Anderson, 1999; Rosenfeld et al, 2003). Drug dealers, especially those who were younger and engaged in social supply to their peers in the suburbs, worked in cash and they were not necessarily "hardmen", Socko argued. Even those who were ostensibly "tough" were not so tough in comparison to someone like him, who had existing criminal ties back to the notorious south and east sides of the city. Socko himself started dealing drugs and this gave him a better insight into other local players – who had what, who stored what, and when and where shipments and transactions would take place. He explained:

'Shuggie was a good mate of mine. I didn't want to end up like him but, doing a stretch for fucking nothing. I already had a charge dropped for robbery and had community service for an assault ... [I would use] the knowledge I had as to who was getting into the drugs game. I said to my mate to get in on it with me. [I would] give him the details and that was basically that. He would rob them not long after they got what they were getting [drugs].'

Socko's intention was to sit back and work behind the scenes while others did his doing, but occasionally he got his hands dirty because he found a life of crime fun. Eventually this would be his downfall, leading to incarceration for his part in a robbery:

'I liked the excitement it gave. It is like a pure buzz … I went with my big mate. It was only a nine bar [nine ounces of weed] the boy had got. Was nothing, to be fair. Prob not even worth it but it was something to do, and money is money, eh … After we took the nine bar, the boy said, "I know it is you", like he knew me. Said my name, so that was me fucked. He was a gimp, but you're not wanting it getting about that you are robbing the boys you are selling to. I pulled my scarf down and was right up in his [face], saying, "You want fucking doo'd, eh". I lost it and stabbed him, didn't I … I took his car. Was fucked up. He reported it and we was done for the robbery. The charge was theft of the vehicle.'

Fraser, like Socko, observed a general shift towards robbing drug dealers as people matured and needed money and commercial robbery became too risky. Yet Fraser, unlike Socko, was not involved in robbery that often and other than spending time engaging in opportunistic robbery during his mid-teens as a somewhat therapeutic coping mechanism for the traumatizing robbery experiences he himself had suffered, he quickly ceased such acts as he got older. Much like Chris had been present when Fraser committed his first robbery, however, Fraser was often on the scene when people he knew opportunistically robbed others. Including once when a drug user robbed another drug user and when a known criminal robbed a retail-level drug dealer Fraser was meant to purchase drugs from:

'I had fuck all to do with any of that. [Paul] just said to [Alex] what had he got after he had been out getting cocaine from [Charlie]. After he told him, he just took it off him and said it was his now. I am mates with [Alex] but I was like, "It is nothing to do with me. You're on your own," and that was all … Aye. I think he just did it cause he could. Wanted it and was simple … [The other occasion] I was with Ricky. We had went along the bridge to meet Socko's mate [Yusuf] to get some green [weed]. A guy we know [Taz] was out and about and seen what was going down. He walked wi' us over the bridge after we bumped into him. We were trying to ditch him cause he is a like a dodgy yain. One that is bad news. But [Yusuf] was right there to meet us and must not have known what Taz was like. He shouts out, "Got that green for you." Taz well clicked on … [Taz took] the green off [Yusuf] and even the money from my mate … he is a heavy psycho. I wasn't going to say nothing over it.'

Fraser's use of the term 'psycho' to describe Taz indicates that he was unpredictable and dangerous. Any attempts to restrain Taz would have resulted in well understood physical consequences. Socko explained that Taz was an older individual, known for robbing drug dealers and drug users, and he gained a fearsome reputation after doing a stint in prison for robbing and repeatedly stabbing a local shopkeeper. This well-publicized attack in the late 1990s left the victim needing life-saving surgery. Taz was not interviewed for this study, but his targeting people on the street after serving time for robbing a shop and getting caught on CCTV may indicate he too changed tactics to attack more vulnerable targets than legal businesses and 'innocent victims'. Collectively, these narratives support the idea that even when driven by drug addiction or financial stress, robbing drug dealers and users, especially at the lower end of the market, carried far less repercussions than robbing traditional targets, and for early-career drug dealers still learning the rules of the road, robbery was a very real threat.

Concluding remarks

As outlined earlier, robbery in Glasgow and West Scotland has evolved with time. With heightened security and the expansion of the illicit drugs market, robbery today revolves around the illegal sphere, and in particular drug dealers and users. Participant Goldsmith touched on this process stating that at the crossroads of change, in the 1980s, the professional criminal class were given two options if they wished to continue a life in crime: (1) abandon predatory-based crimes such as bank robbery, and instead become involved in market-based organized crime such as drug trafficking and distribution; or (2) to continue to engage in predatory-based crimes like robbery, but shift the focus from robbing legitimate institutions to robbing illegitimate ones, namely the people involved in the lucrative drugs trade. Similar changes were observed at the lower level of the criminal hierarchy. After Socko and Fraser witnessed the reputational and occupational risks of petty theft and commercial robbery they moved on to robbing drug dealers.

THREE

The Will to Rob

This chapter draws upon the voices of our participants to explore some of the reasons why robbery occurs within Scotland's illicit drugs trade. Some motivations are somewhat obvious given the victim-offender overlap and relationship to the law, the potential profits involved, the accessibility of targets, and so on, yet some motivational factors are not so obvious and require deeper contextual analysis. While the chapter aims to discuss robbery in the drugs markets specifically, many of the motivations discussed can be applied to robbery in general (for example Jacobs and Wright, 1999; Contreras, 2012).

Robbing for money ... and what money can buy

Compared to high-end market-based crimes like drugs-, firearms-, and sex-trafficking, robbery provides instant gratification. Usually all that is needed is the willingness to "go ahead" and "get stuck in" when the opportunity presents itself, interviewees said. If done right, the financial rewards can be great because what sets robbery apart from similar predatory-based crimes like theft or burglary is the instant cash – there is less need to work with third parties to store and sell stolen goods. The money is therefore the main reason why our interviewees started robbing. Participant Stephen told us simply: "I do it for money. Really, I do, do it for the money".

Stephen robbed for the money, but money was never an end unto itself. Money was a means to achieve something else. To pay household bills, buy a house, a car, or other luxury goods, even go on holiday. Another interviewee, Dicky, took the pragmatic view that robbery with any motive was primarily fuelled by one's need to self-indulge: "Why does anyone do anything now? Self-indulgence, you know." Money satisfied this need by affording the offender the means to purchase whatever is "one's poison".

Stephen commented that robbery could bring almost instant-aneous changes in fortune. One minute, he was indebted or struggling to pay for goods and services, and then, one robbery later, he was back on track and his worries were in the rear-view mirror. It was the instant gratification that robbery provided, the (financial) stress relief, that drove Stephen to rob.

Other interviewees spoke to us about needing money to service their addictions – gambling, sex, and their curated self. Rocky, who is a bodybuilding enthusiast, for example, committed robbery to maintain his image. At over 6 feet tall and weighing 280 lbs (approximately 127 kg), Rocky states:

'Looking like this is not something that happens overnight. It take years, years, of training, mate. Years of dedication … Like I said, I have always trained … Cardio training, then the bodybuilding. Shifted to strength training, say, late 20s, and back to hypertrophy [enlargement of muscle tissue], about 32. It is constant. [It can take] years to [build muscle], and weeks, no kidding, weeks, to lose it. Can all go, bang [clicks fingers], like that. Then back to training again. The juice [steroids] help[s]. Everyone thinks, inject this or swallow that and the muscle packs on. It doesn't. [Steroids] help the muscle grow, helps repair, faster. Retain a lot of fluid. But need to [consume steroids] prop, know, do it properly. In cycles over a couple of weeks, then off. Only use the cycles when at them points, those hard points that [I cannot] get past [without steroids]. Everyone has their points. I struggled to get over 12.7 stones, then again at 15.6, and again at 18. I don't stay on the juice, course not, scrambles your brain. They are not cheap. The eating is a fortune. I spend over a grand a month on food for myself alone for clean eating. The products can cost an arm. I get some stuff for free, know, through contacts in the [bodybuilding] scene. The isolate and concentrated whey, I buy. The creatine I buy, vit[amine]s, supplements. It is expensive … I feel I have to only wear the latest [fashion]. I laze around in tracksuit bottoms in the house, but even then I guess it is still top of the range. Way I am thinking, is no point in getting pumped, but running around in rags … I work part-time, rest of money comes from the lifting. [That is how] I sometimes get in trouble, maybe I need money, so taking from [local street dealers] gives that extra money I need, get what I am saying, mate? I couldn't care what is done, not by who. I need money, [taking money by force] brings that.'

As perhaps evident from Rocky's statement, from the precise nature of his weight points to his knowledge of anabolic steroids, his daily life revolves around bodybuilding. This hobby, in Rocky's own words, has become an "obsession" or addiction that he cannot break with. Case in point: Rocky only works part-time because working full-time eats into his training regime. This, in turn, eats into Rocky's legitimate income.

Rocky's physique is expensive – the gym membership, drugs, and supplements, all cost money. And a great body needs great clothes to show it off, so Rocky thinks nothing of spending thousands on high-end designer clothing. Rocky trains hard, eats healthy, and even robs petty street dealers, all in the name of bodybuilding. But Rocky robs street dealers for a reason – they're soft targets. By operating locally, Rocky uses his local reputation as a "solid" individual and ample "fighter" to intimidate dealers primarily through threats. Rocky states that he rarely has to use force because of his size and aggressive demeanour, and because he picks on the guys at the bottom of the ladder there are rarely any consequences.

For Rocky, robbing drug dealers was about supporting a lifestyle choice, which had addictive traits. One practitioner we interviewed, Murray, observed how the need for young men to look good was increasingly becoming the motivation for a crime like robbery:

'[How] young men define themselves [in the West of Scotland] has changed quite significantly over the last ten years or so. At the turn of the century, Scotland, and in particular, in and around the city of Glasgow, young men would define their identity with an "I don't give a fuck" kind of attitude, and who is the biggest personality, or the toughest. Following deindustrialization, chances to show this kind of masculinity through work begin to disappear. As such, it, of course, found other outlets. On the streets this is manifested through violence, through fighting, and through risk-taking with anti-social behaviour. How else can young boys show their masculinity and define themselves in areas which have nothing, are dilapidated, and parents who may be second or even third generation unemployed? ... Violence is important for saying who they are, but not for the younger generation. They are much more defined by this neoliberal, leisure-based society. They are what they have, what they wear. This has coincided with more parental debt to clothe the kids, more drug dealing to sustain extra needed income, and taking care of themselves. A knife scar was once a source of pride and status. Not now. It is just seen as ugly by today's teenagers. The change in how males in Scotland define and identify themselves, between today's teenagers from yesterday's young adults, is dramatic, to say the least.'

Coming from an academic background, and with over two decades of experience in youth work, Murray provided considerable insight into the changing nature of masculine identity and performance in Glasgow and West Scotland like something out of Winlow's (2001) 'Badfellas'. Still, some addictions never change.

For our interviewees Billy and Chris, robbery was about chasing a high. Billy described a "perfect storm" of addictions driving his robbery career – gambling and drugs:

> 'I was bad on the coke at the time. I was snorting, saying roughly, a gram or two each day, even at work. It just felt constant. I had a decent wage from [company name], the [job] paid well, aye. Paid well for my age, then. I could afford [to do so]. I was selling the gear [cocaine] on the side. [First], mostly to mates, and it just rolled from there a bit. More I was going to dancing, stuff. Made sense to punt [cocaine and ecstasy] then … gambling was a heavy issue. Hadn't always been right bad, bad, but I think taking the lines was fucking wi' my brain. Start thinking stupidly. If I was down [from gambling] would make me feel total shite … then, would be erratic, pure paranoid … started to [rob] the boys I was meeting to sell [drugs] to. Size them [up]. If they didn't know me, I didn't know them. I would take their money … [To fund my] gambling … at one time I must have been putting, uft, easy must have been, say, easy a few hundred a day into the roulette. Maybe about 300 a day over a few weeks. I would win, go back [and put] everything in, right back in.'

Billy's partner-in-crime Chris, added sex to this list of vices:

> 'I wouldn't say I was a proper robber, masked on, [shotgun] in hand, blasting away [laughs]. Billy was really the one doing that, you know. I was with him, aye, sure.

Happened to be there. Maybe get into character, get me. Aye, I played the part, full of it [laughs] … I took my share. Billy would just split it. [I had a] problem with hookers, man … Was working away … in the digs [so] get heavy boring. Was paying for escorts. It is, well, not now, it was a problem for a wee bit there … [money we robbed] was spent on the hookers. Was a regular in that [strip club] by 19, man.'

While the drugs were not the *primary* reason for engaging in robbery, they certainly distorted Billy's thinking, and give Chris the confidence to act alongside his associate, firstly to sell drugs, and later to meet individuals as potential drugs customers who could be sized up and, if the setting was right, robbed. Billy and Chris' participation in the drugs market introduced them to the crime of robbery – it gave them the opportunity and resources to do the crime, emboldened by the fact that the nature of some transactions meant that buyers and sellers had no prior contact and victims could not go to law enforcement anyway.

The highs and lows of gambling were what really drove Billy to commit robbery – a crime, which, as we discuss later, offered similar fundamental thrills to gambling. For Chris, it was his friendship with Billy. Chris merely 'played the part' of a robber, yet was fully aware of Billy's intent, thus was still culpable. Indeed, Billy would 'split' the money, suggesting this was a joint venture. Billy spent the money on escorts and prostitutes, another source of instantaneous thrill that Chris had developed some form of dependency on from his time working away from home.

Psychopharmacological and economic-compulsive robbery

One addiction conspicuous by its absence from the earlier section was drug addiction. In a seminal paper, Goldstein

(1985) argued drugs and crime were linked in three ways: the psychopharmacological (that is, drug intoxication facilitates violence), the economically compulsive (that is, drug users commit crime to finance their drug use), and the systemic (that is, crime is integral to the illegal drug distribution market because it affords no legal way of obtaining justice when rules are violated). This section focuses on the first two concepts.

Prior studies have documented an association between drug addiction and robbery, especially in the hard drug economy (see Jacobs, 2000; Casey et al, 2009; Harding et al, 2019). Coomber (2006) points out that many heroin and (crack) cocaine suppliers are themselves addicts or users, primed for victimization. Not all drug users are problem users, many are simply recreational users (McPhee et al, 2019; Hart, 2021). As Casey et al (2009) observe, however, the minority of problematic users cause disproportionate harm to the community and are responsible for an inordinate amount of crime. One of our interviewees, Darren, observed:

> **D**: I couldn't prove it, but I know more folk robbed for drugs, or by cunts mad on the drugs, I do, than other people who have just robbed folk, or robbed liked the shops. Even [my local shop] got robbed, literally a few days ago. [It was a] raving crack addict. Stole [cigarettes], money, course, a few sandwiches from the fridge [laughs].
>
> **I**: *Why the sandwiches?*
>
> **D**: Would have been wanting money for [drugs]. Sandwich probably cause he would be needing a serious feed, you know [laughs]. [Addicts are] always in need of food [because they spend] their money [on drugs].

Another interviewee, Gavin, was adamant that "trouble started when I started taking drugs". Even before the drugs, however, was alcohol:

'I have spent about half of my adult life in jail. I would say that it was drugs that really got me into trouble. I was in high school when I started taking drugs. I wouldn't touch heroin. I have to admit I was surprised I ended up taking heroin. My aunt was a heroin addict and she was fucked. I never liked her because of it and never wanted to be like her. I would take ecstasy, Valium, jellies with drink. I would take LSD when I left school with my outside [of school] pals. I started smoking when I was about 12. I started smoking cannabis when I was about 12. At the same time. I did one and started doing the other. Everything else I started after that like ecstasy. I would drink. I would save up my pocket money and not eat at lunch. I was meant to [take the money and] go to [the local café] and get lunch. I would save it and get drunk at the weekend with the money instead. I would buy Buckfast [fortified wine with caffeine] because it got you hefty steaming. Sometimes I would buy Merrydown [super strength cider]. I would buy Mad Dog [MD 20/20, American fortified wine], the orange bottle. I hated the Red and Green that came out later.'

Gavin went on to argue it was under the influence of drink and drugs that he started offending:

'I got my first offence for vandalism. Me and my mate were outside drunk and decided to smash a few car windows for a laugh. We got carried away and I think we broke into and set on fire around 28 cars that night. It must be some kind of record. We broke into a car dealers as well and set the cars on fire in the place and pushed them into the wee river … I got into a stolen car [a month] later and drove it drunk over a roundabout and lost my licence. I only had it about a week lol. Me and my mate then took another car a month later going to pick up some lassies and were drunk and the car tyre blew and we went through a wall. It was a historical wall so made the papers. I got charged for that. And after all of that I lost my apprenticeship and cause the outstanding cases and no licence and then the criminal record I couldn't get any work. I started doing more drugs then and started to sell them to my mate's wee brother and his pals. They were punting [selling[the drugs we were giv[ing] them but I wasn't doing it for profit, just to help [my] mate's brothers.'

It wasn't long before Gavin graduated to robbery:

'I then met Steve and we started breaking into shops and doing insurance jobs. We were also fighting with this other team but at the time because they didn't like where we stayed beside their scheme. Me and Steve got the jail for fighting against them one night and one of their boys got stabbed. A few months later I was out and then got the jail again for "macheting" Steve and another mate over a daft argument. I then pulled away from them and started hanging about with some other boys that stayed close by that I knew from when I stayed in town. We started to sell quite a bit of drugs and eventually I got the jail for that as well. I was charged over a fight that broke out which was to do with what we were doing and I got the jail with my other mate for battering some boy. I had a few other wee charges as well and I also had a robbery of a local bookies. Wasn't a proper robbery. I smashed the place up and then took money from some of the customers and the police came and battered me and I got the jail for it. I was in prison again and then got out after a few months. It might have been a year. I got longer but didn't do the full stretch.'

Gavin explained that a lot of guys he hung out with at this time were retail-level drug dealers and that gave him the idea of robbing them:

'Not heavy, but they always sold drugs. The place is known for being a place that you get drugs because every [other] tenement has a dealer living in it. We just started robbing them. We would rib them after we battered them if they started the fight. If they jumped us and battered us then we knew who they were and would go back to get them later and would break into their houses, or get them when they were going out to the shops and stuff, and we would batter them with bats, sock and brick, or sometimes knives. We would take their money and their drugs if they were dealers or drug users … We started robbing them and hitting where it hurts, taking their drugs then they would stop coming for us. Because they sold drugs it was easy to say it is okay to take their drugs and money because it is drug money. I also took drugs still now and then, so it was helping me to get drugs when I needed [a fix]. This happened when stressed. When guys are after you in the place you stay it makes stress.'

Gill, a former heroin addict, described for us how drug addicts often found themselves caught in cycles of robbery offending, but also victimization:

'[I had developed] a bit of a [drug] habit. Was heroin. Mostly smoked it then … the local boys had been robbing. The guy I was then running with, he was an addict, an older guy. A proper addict … injecting … I see taking stuff from other people just as easy … [I had been] charged with breaking and entering. [I had] broken into the chemist on the High Street. It was jail bait. Starts this swinging door in and out of jail and it is no good. You are dry [drug-free] then out and back on the gear. Back in and dry. Out again and on it. So, you are detoxing on and off and on. I thought if I took gear off people I knew that sold it … They can't go to police. A lot of people in them circles were [robbing from] other people in them circles, dealers and users doing each other over. Yes, it draws less attention. It was more, you would say successful at the time … It is kept in house. Course it is deceitful. Isn't nice, but I justified it saying they are game, they are drug users. Addicts. They would fuck me over. Yeah, they were mostly other addicts.'

Habitual drug use and overwhelming drug debts were at the forefront of most of the opportunistic low-level robberies in our study. Jason, who at the time of interview had abused drugs for over three decades, spoke about how he first developed a drug habit:

'Growing up, mate, I [had] never been [into] getting out my face. I rarely drunk, mate, hardly knew anything about drugs. Mate, I couldn't [have told] you this drug from that. If I went back, back in time the now, and I was to ask the people in my [school] class[room] if they thought I was going to do well, am sure most would have said, "Aye, mate". Spot on. [After leaving school and securing an apprenticeship] I did make good money, mate, oh, aye, real good. I always had money to spend on what I wanted. Carried a wad in my jacket, rolled up like this [demonstrates], after payday at end of the week … My mates, aye, in Govan, me and them, we weren't like bad folk, no, mate, more have a good time. You know, mate … I did start to drink a bit then, few mates [smoked weed]. Best mucker Davie B had started getting into [heroin]. Few mates started and so did I. Just to try it, know, mate? We never thought it was, the way you might, people do now, like dirty. People didn't. No then, no like initially, no. That is how it started out … I hadn't been a wrong one, never liked trouble [or] fighting.'

From that first high on heroin, things changed quickly for Jason and once his life hit rock bottom, he turned to robbery to relieve the physical, emotional, and economic pressures of his addiction:

'I had good money and could sustain my addiction, at first, aye, mate, [but my] family life was like fucking up, mate, doing more [heroin], you see, it gets in the way ... It took everything, [eventually] my [partner] left, took my wee boy. It's shite to say, but I didn't care then, I cared, aye, like I wanted them here, you know, with me, here, but like [I didn't] really care because when you're into an addiction, it is everything and all you really care about. It is you. That addiction is you, it owns you as a person ... I would get clean, then back on it, clean, back, you know how it is. I was 40 before I even got my first conviction. I lost my job and started begging, living on fucking streets, mate ... Still I have morals, wouldn't steal or that, no robbing from old ones. Other guys I was like in their circle with, they would. I never could ... [My addiction] got out of control [after a] big [pay-out from gambling]. I fucked the lot, didn't I? I spent over two and a half grand on [heroin]. A week. In a fucking week. Come on, mate. Giving it out [as well], to supposed mates. Then it's gone. I want it back. I felt that crave, mate, like cause I had been [in] freefall, doing more, aye ... Davie's brother, [Mr S] was around, Davie had died, aye, few years before, [Mr S] was on the game [addict] as well. We got close, through drugs, mate, that is all thinking ... I was like fuck it, man, I need this. Me and [Mr S] went to [Mr D, Mr A, Mr E's] place, well, two places really, cause [Mr E] lived at his maw's still really, but wasn't in when we broke into the house. We took his TV and stereo anyway. Stole money and some rings in the living room. Think they were his mum's ... we went round after that to [Mr D's], aye, and we robbed them, at knifepoint. Me and [Mr S], aye. I was like pure anxious, but I was on a heavy comedown and needed it. I didn't care.'

Jason's experience was consistent with a number of other participants in the study, who first consumed drugs recreationally as adolescents, but fell into a cycle of addiction that lasted well into adulthood. Eventually, Jason's need to consume heroin became so intense it dominated his thinking and completely guided his behaviour. Jason's drug use cost him his family – his partner at the time left him. She had experimented with heroin herself, Jason said, but thankfully never developed an addictive relationship with the drug and was able to cease taking it once she fell pregnant with Jason's son.

McPhee et al (2019) argue that despite popular conceptions and stereotypes, although some drugs such as heroin are shown to have more addictive properties, not everyone who takes heroin will instantly become an addict, and in fact many can and do consume the drug recreationally. For Jason this was not the case, and after a "big" £2,500 win at the local bookies, he lost whatever self-control he still had and spent all of his winnings on heroin for himself and friends. Two and a half thousand pounds on drugs in a week. Consuming so much so quickly only increased his tolerance for the drug and pushed Jason's need to consume further. Following a "heavy comedown", he and his friend, who had, according to Jason, always been involved in petty crime, decided to break into the homes of their friends and rob them at knifepoint. This cycle of sustaining one's habit then losing control was common among research participants who had addictions or addictive personalities. It was during the worst periods of addiction that they tended to engage in more risky crimes, especially robbery.

Ronald is perhaps the definition of a career criminal. He told us:

'First stretch [prison sentence] was car theft. Second time [in prison], hmm, that was, assault, aye, assault. I came out and went back in for theft, well, stealing from a shop, M&S [Marks & Spencer], and I battered the security guard over the head with a bottle of vodka I took. That was the Paisley Centre, well, outside it, aye. That was all the Young Offenders, Polmont [Prison], I was sent to. I got moved to [Barlinne], was out a few weeks and then went back in for breaking early release conditions … I stabbed a guy … was in again for assault. Out. Then I got a few years for a robbery and assault. Think I might have been jailed for smashing up William Hill after that, maybe before, mate. No after. Then I was last in again for armed robbery … Aye, could say that, aye, [I] was a bit of a rascal.'

While he was no angel from the beginning, Ronald argued that drug addiction was behind his worst robbery escapades:

'I didn't have a drug habit till I went in for stabbing that guy I said about. Was just shite, going nowhere, absolutely nowhere. Inside you want to pass time, so just try and get the head down, know. Take sleepers to help, what else am I going to do? Stare at walls, fuck sake. I was using heroin then, aye … [once released and now with a heroin habit] I would just steal shit. I was punting [selling] as well. Like sell heroin to cover my own use. You get me … Aye, sometimes [my addiction would] run away from me. More when I was feeling pure shite about shit, you use more, aye. Then I would have the debt as well. The guy I was getting from said, "Debt's too much, nae mere [no more] for you." You know what am saying. It leaves you right up shit creek. Needing a fix and needing money to pay for [previous] fixes … See no getting a fix when you're needing one. It can be heavy going, like in your brain and that. My body was actually sore … that's when I would be more likely to be doing them robberies … for about three maybe five weeks, man, I was just on the run out robbing people. Going fucking wild. Thing is, I knew I would get the jail but I was in that [moment], no are

not living for the future, man, it's all the here and now.
Acting pure brash.'

Ronald accumulated drug debts whenever his habit
overwhelmed him. He then felt additional pressure to pay for
previous consumption, as well as immediate consumption, and
this fuelled robbery sprees in which he performed multiple
armed robberies at knifepoint. Ronald said that his insatiable
appetite for heroin, combined with other stresses, impaired
his judgement and rational thinking capacity, forcing him to
go "wild".

Drugs lower inhibitions, but somewhat contrary to the
stereotype of economic-compulsive crime, Ronald felt he was
more likely rob others, not when intoxicated, but when he was
"drying out" from drugs and "in need of a fix". In this context, Ronald would engage in increasingly risky behaviour to
feed his addiction and alleviate, even if only momentarily, the
emotional and physical pain associated with heroin withdrawal:

'[I]t was a pure big problem for me. I would pure do
anything for that hit, man. It is strange, man, unless you
have been there you can't really explain it. Even now
I can't actually understand why I would do what I did
… The fear of not getting a [hit], makes you think daft
thoughts. I was already thinking pure daft … because
I was an addict, man. It is the fear of being dry. It is a fear.
I would ache … I've [done] hold-ups … I slashed [Mr
D] at his door, in front of his kids, right in front of them,
as well, wasn't feeling good about it … for a tenner bag
[of heroin]. Robbed, stole from my own mum and dad,
stepdad, but you know. [Addiction] pure took over my
life. I looked like shite, man … the need for drugs but,
I would think, "I am robbing this guy" and I could have
known him since I was a kid. I would steal my oldest
kid's pocket money. I would always think I will get it
back to him, but never did of course.'

Prior research has similarly found that in crack cocaine markets, addicts were most likely to take risks when they were searching for their next high (for example Jacobs, 2000). Ronald was clear that other drug users would do the same to him as he had done to them under the influence of drug intoxication or the fear of drug withdrawal. There were blurred lines between offender and victim, which was also true for drug dealers, who were even bigger targets.

Debt and debt-bondage as motives for robbery

A number of participants also spoke about owing drug debt as a motivational factor for engaging in robbery. Richard, for example, had fallen on hard times. He had just done time for commercial robbery and was making an effort to "go straight" upon release. But as is common in the lives of career criminals (Ezell and Cohen, 2005; Maruna, 2001), his desistence ebbed and flowed and he drifted in and out of offending because it was all he could do to survive. Richard described to us being "pulled into" armed robbery owing to the company he kept and old vendettas and debts that were never fully resolved:

> 'Why did I do it? Suppose I needed the money. I had not been involved in literally anything since the last time I had been out [and released from prison]. Going straight isn't like that's it I am never doing anything again. Kind of like I am okay for a while, and then out and about and get pulled into whatever have you. That last time [I committed robbery], I felt [as] though, I had been chasing my tail for a fair bit, aye. Like I needed to get on top again. Weird, I didn't feel the same on the last rob. Maybe [be]cause it was purely for money.'

Dean, who had himself been a drug dealer, likewise fell on hard times financially following some poor business decisions. He purchased a large bulk of drugs with cash in advance from a trusted source, only to be told that due to "unforeseen circumstances", the shipment would not arrive. The story was the drugs were seized by the police, but for obvious reasons Dean could never verify that and he was suspicious he'd been cheated. Dean was left with no money and no drugs and no way to recuperate his losses:

> 'Was kind of fucked. I wasn't happy, pal, no. I had paid for it. Thought I could trust him. Gave 6,500 upfront, and had already put down a deposit to get the order. Some rubbish about it going elsewhere if I couldn't get the 500 down. Who knows. Likely rubbish. I phoned her, "Where the fuck is my [drugs]?", "Eh, oh, eh, hm, it was take[n]." Aye, whatever, she pocketed it. I know it.'

In an effort to make himself whole, Dean robbed a close associate of his source. He was successful, thus emboldened to track down his source and retrieve the rest of his money, with interest, for the troubles he received:

> 'I couldn't find her. Had vanished. [She had] fucked over a number [of people] from what I had heard ... I got her brother, but it's nothing to do wi' him. Got back a couple of hundred. Though, am sure he actually paid out of sympathy cause he said he knew what she was like.'

Dean saw his actions as simply retrieving money owed to him, but the fact was he had become an accidental robber.

Other participants spoke about engaging in robbery in an effort to obtain fast money, and given contacts in the criminal underworld, they were able to identify 'easy' targets who had money stored, and were themselves lacking in criminal prestige as being 'hard men' or having the capability to retaliate effectively. Often the need to acquire vast sums quickly was tied to outstanding debts, and in the case of Alan, bills that had accumulated while he was incarcerated. These debts had acquired significant interest from the lender, a criminal them-selves, over time:

> 'Having done five years in [HM Prison], I got out …
> I get a visit out the blue. [Criminal A] and his cronies,
> [Criminal B] and [Criminal C], think that was his name,
> [the] youngest … [You] owe us 15 large [£15,000]. Fuck,
> come on, where the fuck am I going to get that? [I had
> only been out] a short spell. I said about having been
> inside the nick [prison], no like I have cash laying around.
> Anything saved is spent by the misses while inside. Still
> have children to raise, [in the] nick or not. They knew
> that, but chancing it. Lucky I didn't have them fucking
> shot, pricks. [But they] gave me an address, said I was
> to pay a visit [and it] would be made right, know. [The]
> boy inside [the address given] was a quiet one, a gobshite,
> nothing more. [They told me] he was holding up 20
> grand. Had heard it, aye, but this was solid, they're saying.
> [I was to] give them the 15. Square it off. Anything else
> I should keep as a start-up … I did it, aye. Was closer to
> about three grand more.'

Alan states that his potential assailants exploited his situation, blaming him for the drugs and firearm seized during a police raid years before. This was the crime Alan had served time for, but time served was not enough for these guys. The debtors wanted Alan to pay back what he owed, with interest. They presented an 'opportunity' for him to do so with the added incentive of a financial bonus, but Alan really had no choice otherwise because violence would result if he refused. Alan was well aware his robbing this up-and-coming drug dealer was part of his assailants' plan to get ahead in the drugs game and put a rival out of business for a while. This would ensure customers and clientele came their way instead. Any potential repercussions in the meantime would come Alan's way, and not theirs. It would therefore seem that the motivations for robbery can often share considerable similarities, and while differences may be minute, they can have profoundly different effects for those involved.

When 'the action is the juice'

There is a noteworthy scene in the 1995 movie *Heat*, directed by Michael Mann, where a team of bank robbers debates whether or not the next heist is worth the risk. When one character is advised to sit out the crime because the heat is on and he doesn't need the money, he famously quips: "Well, you know, for me, the action is the juice." This one line captures perfectly what Katz (1988) calls, the 'seductions of crime'.

While monetary rewards and consumption habits tended to be the main, or overarching, reasons for committing robbery among our sample, other factors played an important role in sustaining robbery careers. As evident from some of the prior statements of participants like Dean and Chris, there was a prevalent and consistent undertone to the data, which suggests robbery is at least motivated in part by emotions, thrill-seeking, 'the buzz', and the social status attached to being a criminal. As Alan told us:

'No [going to] spout this and that, [or] be saying it isn't a buzz, mate, you know what I mean? You're in there and holding up the place with a shooter [gun]. Course, you get a kick from it all. Suppose it is natural, you get me? … I always do that bit more than I need to I think. Like I enjoy the risk of not getting away with it. Not actually, not making it, [but] the feeling from the thought, "Oh, fuck me". It is a rush, know, suppose. Making [the robbery that] wee smudge more harder is a bit more a buzz, of excitement, aye, you know what I mean? … I know boys that say they get a hard-on [an erection]. I always need to bang out a shite, but, mind you, instead [laughs]. Makes me nervous, a good [nervous] from it, still.'

It is evident from Alan's statement that some individuals feel as though they need to continuously place themselves in a state of danger or risk, where success and failure are clearly in the balance, just to feel like they accomplished something worthwhile. People like Alan need that "rush" to feel alive but it's the rush that gets so many robbers in trouble; they take unnecessary risks and fail to quit while they're ahead. Think back to when Ricky was robbed in Chapter One. The robbers got paid with relative ease, but one of them felt compelled to hit Ricky after the fact. This caused Ricky to fight back and in the end it's a miracle no one was killed.

Alan states that the excitement generated by the act of robbery can for some people replicate the feeling of sexual arousal, with similar physical consequences. For others, like Alan, it can all become too much and result in needing to, or at least feeling like they need to, go to the toilet. Other participants spoke about overwhelming physical reactions to robbery such as nausea and vomiting, feeling light-headed, even physically shaking: a consequence of the natural fight-or-flight reaction and the adrenaline coursing through their veins. During the robbery itself, however, participants said they felt "in the zone" and some claimed to experience a higher state of consciousness. Time seemed to slow down and their senses were heightened. As Alan explained:

'It is as though it slows, mate, going that slow mo. You play the game [Grand Theft Auto 3] for the PlayStation? I am not that into games but I know your lot are. My boy, well, ex-bird's wee boy. We weren't married but I call him my boy, know. We are close. He would play it. I played it with him ... when the lad's busting into the room and shooting it up on the computer, you can press the slow mo[tion] button on it, or it might be a wee drink you take, like the items, cannot mind now. Think, it is a drink [or] drugs your boy takes in the game, you know what I mean but don't you? Aye? Aye. It goes that slow way

[and] your wee computer guy can see everything that [bit] slower. You can zoom in and make the bad guys you're popping shots at that clearer way. Well, that is [how I would] describe [doing a robbery] if I had to. Something like that. [It] feels like it is going that bit slower [but in reality] is happening pure fast. [My eyesight improves during robbery], it is the only time I don't need to wear my glasses. Think I am kidding? I'm blind 99 per cent of the time. I am [robbing] and my eyes are like the bottom of ginger bottles, pure magnified.'

For Alan, robbery was an experience like no other; it heightened his senses, even improved his poor eyesight to the extent that his glasses and contact lenses were no longer required. Whereas others robbed to feed their addictions, for Alan, robbery was itself addictive. Alan's need to "feel alive" explained why he struggled to hold down a regular job and any serious relationship. He was a womanizer and enjoyed "the thrill of cheating too much". Like Billy, he also had a gambling problem, and like Fraser, in his younger days he would actively engage in gang fights or engage in other risky behaviour such as carrying weapons or venturing into rival territory alone or with the odds stacked firmly against him and his peers. Robbery was an extension of this thrill-seeking behaviour and the way it manifested itself in the criminal sphere of Alan's life.

Concluding remarks

This chapter explored some of the motivations behind robbery in drug markets. Robbery is rife in this context because drug dealers and consumers are easy targets; they carry drugs and money and have little recourse to the law. At the same time, however, those involved in robbery are often themselves caught up in drug supply, use, or abuse. While this gives robbers a competitive edge, such as the necessary insight into committing crime successfully, they too are vulnerable, often forced into taking unnecessary risks. In truth, robbery is fuelled by a desire to acquire money and frequently also drugs, whether to feed habits large and small or to settle debts and scores. Yet, emotions, such as the need to take risks, seek excitement, and chase the buzz, play an important part in sustaining one's robbery career beyond the occasional act.

FOUR

Robbery in Action

The title of this chapter deliberately harks back to Wright and Decker's (1997a) classic examination of armed robbers 'in action', because like them, we seek to use our conversations to account for offenders' decision-making in relation to robbery, explore how and why targets are chosen, and detail the various tactics used in a robbery. While the term 'robbery' conjures up images of polished and professional gangsters doing 'business' (Hobbs, 1988, 1995), at times the crime can be rather perfunctory. This is particularly true at the very bottom end of the trade where most robberies are poorly planned, if planned at all, and mostly opportunistic, perpetrated against anyone from weekend drinkers and clubbers to young people who are out shopping alone. In Glasgow and West Scotland, robbery is so common that it is almost routine, but as the targets get harder, namely wholesale drug dealers at the middle and upper levels of the illicit drugs trade, then robberies become more sophisticated and involve greater preparation and resources.

Minor drug dealers become targets for robbery when they are seen to have hard currency on them, and when the circumstances are right, they can be easy pickings, with little repercussions. However, robbery at the lower level of the illicit drugs trade is not just about drugs and money, but status rewards and humiliating rivals and victims for thrills and 'kicks'. This perhaps explains why one reoccurring theme from the interviews was that dealings at this level often caused the most trouble and were highly problematic. This was for a host of reasons consistent with the idea of 'bounded rationality' (Cornish and Clarke,

1986), including: offenders just starting out and having little practical experience; offenders not anticipating or considering all alternatives and all information; offenders not knowing or not trusting one another, with relationships, business partnerships, and interactions with other criminals still in the embryotic stages of development; and desperate actors taking unnecessary risks because they have nothing to lose.

This chapter examines the performance and practice of robbery, including how victims are selected and how risks are managed or not.

Victim selection and the 'performance' of robbery

Robbery can be conducted by a single attacker, but more commonly it is conducted in a 'gang' or group context with other people present. The manifest reasoning here is that there is strength in numbers and many hands make light work. Having an audience can also boost the status rewards of the crime. Some group members are present but passive while the robbery takes place, whereas others are active participants in the crime. This may include scouting for potential victims, such as young adults of a similar age leaving pubs at night and heading out to nightclubs, targeted because they were intoxicated, ill-prepared and unaware, and assumed to be carrying cash. As Rocky explained:

'We would [go to Glasgow city centre] for a [gang fight] … [but we'd] make a tidy wee earner [in addition] … would wander around the main streets, usually where the old [nightclubs] would be. [Clubgoers] would have to pass … We would rob them [as they] made their way … Cops and adults never got involved either … was easy enough. We were already [in Glasgow] for a [fight] so everyone was usually [carrying weapons] and [intoxicated]. We would all be egging each other to do shit … We would look for stragglers, or goons [weak] …

[We] would just stop them and say, "Gi[v]e's a pound",
but we'd take everything … Anything I got I kept …
Everyone [in the gang] just got in a frenzy and would
be robbing people all over the street.'

In this context, robbery was a type of performance played out
in front of peers to demonstrate bravado and adherence to
group or peer norms. The crime helped strengthen bonds and
a sense of belonging at the group level while individual gang
members built their personal brands and biographies (Harding,
2014). The night's events, in turn, became exaggerated stories
and narratives that contributed to the gang's myth-making
capabilities (Decker and van Winkle, 1996; Pickering et al,
2012; Lauger, 2014).

While the crime described by Rocky appeared highly opportunistic and sporadic, crimes like these served as a training
ground for youth gang members, giving them the confidence
needed to carry out more audacious robbery crimes. Indeed,
some robberies of the general public required a far greater
degree of planning and premeditation, even travel to new
locations to conduct crime, as Boab explained:

'Would travel into town. Just get the bus, you know …
get off and walk through to the Trongate, down to the
Barras.[1] You know, … there's like a wee underpass just off
the main road … was more people about to choose from,
plus no one knows you. If you do shit in your scheme,
you are going to get well huckled [caught by police].'

As Boab points out, with his peers, he would specifically travel
to a certain location at the edge of Glasgow centre, select a
concealed location close to a busy main road, and strategically
target his victims:

'Aye, prob[ably] is a type you look for. No even thinking
about it, mate. You can see when someone is quiet, makes

it easier to take their money, know, man… no' like you're going to take on the guy built like a brick shithouse, and scars all over his coupon [face] … mostly quiet boys themselves, or wi' like one mate or that … Rob junkies as well, they fight back but never go to the police.'

Boab selected his victims based on certain criteria, including their physical appearance and attributes and use of social space, but for Boab this decision-making felt almost natural or unconscious. He looked for people who were "quiet" and less likely to fight back or report to police. Use of the term "boys" indicates his targets were usually younger, thus he had a physical and emotional advantage.

Ronald, who we met earlier, typically robbed people when he was under the influence of drugs and searching for his next high, but when asked him about *who* he robbed, Ronald disclosed there was still some method to his madness:

'Anyone really. Course, it's no[t] like, grabbing people randomly in the street and robbing them. Could tell, an eye out for who was easy prey and who wasn't. In that frame of mind but, when needing to get [heroin immediately] I might take more risks and take on people that are more, say capable … I mostly robbed other users. Was just they were more going to have, you know, heroin on them, or the money for it. No like randoms. It was people I knew, know, knew of them at least a bit, no pal, pals, people just being around the, that, scene. I would be like, "All right, Jamie," that was one of the guys I robbed. "You got anything, mate?", he said. "No, mate, but am going to get a score from a guy I know." I just said would his guy hook me up [as well], then I waited till he got his other mate and I took out my blade and put it to his throat and took his money and his mate's [as well]. I was stupid, course am going to see him again but no thinking straight. The week I got caught I was waiting down at [Lover's Lane] cause it was w[h]ere the dealer stayed, through the park, and loads a guys I know of would walk down through [Lover's Lane] to his house and back. I would jump them on way back after they got brown [heroin].'

While robbery was somewhat indiscriminate, therefore, Ronald targeted some victims intentionally, namely young men and elderly women because they were vulnerable, and other heroin users, who were easily deceived because of his prior knowledge of them in the drugs world. Ronald would pass as just another willing buyer (because he was), luring his peers into a false sense of security. He also timed his attacks to maximize reward and minimize risk.

Once 'in the moment', some offenders adopted a more 'casual approach' (Feeney, 1986) to victim selection, where crude choices were made based on limited information (Jacobs, 2000). Rational choice theorists refer to 'bounded rationality' (Cornish and Clarke, 1986) where time pressures and other factors – in this case, drug addiction – might limit and simplify complex decision-making. In such circumstances, perceived rewards might be exaggerated as justification for risk-taking. Still, brandishing a knife certainly helped Ronald strike fear in his targets and expedite his robberies. This was something we heard from a number of interviewees, such as Steff: "Guys I know [who] rob folk carry blades ... [because] the [victim] will be [more likely] to hand over his stuff ... makes it quick."

Vince explained, however, that carrying a knife was a bit like a self-fulling prophecy, increasing the likelihood that an opportunistic robbery will even occur:

'Not as if I thought I am going take this dagger, rob that cunt, and plug him. Isn't how shit happened. Had the dagger cause [a rival] was pure out scanning the place, [he was] after me. Me and [my friends] bumped into [this rival's] two mates. Things got out of hand, didn't they! We cornered them … made them hug each other, shit, like gays [laughs] … I took the dagger out, [said], "Gees your jackets or you're getting made into a fucking teabag." Thought I was being funny … [probably because] my mates were there. You see your chance, don't you, you take it.'

Taking chances and using weapons were common themes whenever we discussed the motives and methods of robbing drug dealers, which many interviewees described as a 'risky business' (Hutton, 2005). For example, Alan told us:

'Fucking right it's dangerous, man, know? See, you can hit a place and the cunts inside are heavy Ricky Maroo'd [armed] right up, no joke … Aye, we would defo be tooled up. Aye … take a shooter [firearm] if you can get your hands on one … We always had blades, case shit gets close and personal, know … [We] always carried a machete on raids … they aren't the best in truth, mate, but they scare the fuck right out of cunts.'

Prominent displays of weapons capable of producing bodily harm, like firearms and knives, help frighten and intimidate potential victims. Relatedly, a number of our interviewees worked in groups or 'krews' to mitigate risk of reprisals.[2] Ken, a professional armed robber, explained that krews enjoyed "strength in numbers" and could more easily exploit or overwhelm any individual drug dealer. The only problem with group work was the job had to be big enough to make sure everyone got paid. This meant targeting wholesale drug dealers, where the rewards were greater but so too were the risks:

'We would usually steal drugs, aye, mainly drugs, from like other [dealers] … no' like ounces … needs to be worthwhile … that's why we hit it when it's housed [in wholesale quantities], know … depends [upon] who has what, and when they have it, know ... People might know you are into that game but see if they can prove it was you that [robbed] them, they'd wan[t to] fucking kill you, for serious ... Fact, more time goes into planning ... [when] robbing other krews then ramming the locals [shops].'

By targeting more serious criminals, Ken felt more planning and preparation was required, namely to ensure the gang would remain undetected, even when krews are known among criminal networks for practising robbery against other criminals. Robberies were rarely reported to law enforcement unless someone went "too far" and "someone [was] seriously hurt", or if a regular civilian were caught up in any ensuing violence, but if someone was ever identified, Ken said, it could result in victims seeking revenge, even murder.

To mitigate risk, people like Ken who specialized in robbing wholesale drug dealers expressed a preference for hitting them at times and in places where drugs were "housed" and stockpiled. Using intelligence passed on by members of the criminal fraternity, they targeted other criminals' "stash houses" to confiscate cash from drug deals or intended for laundering. As Alan said, however, even the "easy" jobs can go wrong:

'You really want to hit the place when it's empty ... [On one occasion, gang member Zane] was pure mad with it [intoxicated], fucking coked right out his eyeballs ... [He] was [only] to watch the [hostages] ... we use' to always put them in the bathroom crouching down ... It's no[t] like in the movies ... tying cunts up ... No time ... Plus, you start that shit and the cunts are going to fight back. No chance they are going to let you just tie them up ... [Anyway, Zane] starts thinking he has heard one of the guys saying his name, pure para[noid], fucking para, so [he] fucks this cunt right in the head with a hatchet. We had to fucking bail ... left with fuck all [except] an attempted murder wrap on our hands, well, on [his] hands. I wasn't taking no derry [blame] for that.'

While drugs and alcohol could be used to help eliminate fear and 'pump up' Krew members before a robbery, creating 'super-optimism' (Walters, 1990) and a sense of invincibility, it also created new risks. Krew member Zane went too far in this case, nearly killing someone with a hatchet. Zane was punished for his actions. In a revenge attack some months later, Zane was knifed, leaving him with a large scar across his face and head.

Getting played

While the largest and most profitable drug deals occur in networks built on trust at the upper echelons of the market, most drug dealing takes place at retail levels of the market in networks where social ties are weak and trust is fragile. It is perhaps unsurprising to learn that operating in the arena of 'minimally commercial supply' is at time precarious and dealers can take large risks for little reward (Coomber and Moyle, 2014).

Retail-level dealers tend to operate 'solo' or in small partnerships, or occasionally in youth gangs (Windle and Briggs, 2015). The role of gangs in drug sales is well documented (for example Decker and Van Winkle, 1994; Howell and Decker, 1999; McLean et al, 2018) and it's much less risky to enter the drugs market as part of a gang owing to strength in numbers. Still, social suppliers usually operate independently given that drug supply tends to go hand in hand with drug use (Coomber and Moyle, 2014; Fraser, 2015). Having little support in the form of criminal allies leaves such dealers vulnerable to robbery. Dealers have to be on the lookout for customers who are potential robbers, or rival dealers looking to acquire money or goods without paying for them. Harding et al (2019) suggest at this level of the market, and within this context, opportunistic robbery of criminal peers is common and perpetrators often are working alone to 'seize the moment'.

Transactional insecurity was widely recognized among the drug dealing fraternity and accepted as the cost of doing business. William recalls once going to buy drugs and instead casually robbing the dealer: "[I] knew the [dealer] ... [He] stayed [near] me, [and was] a bit younger. [I] heard he was selling [ecstasy tablets] ... I didn't go to rob him, but after I bought the pills I seen him take out a wad of cash and thought, 'Fuck it, am taking that.'"

For William, this robbery was ad hoc and not intended. It resulted from a rapid risk assessment of the situation and the personal attributes of the dealer. William understood where he was and how quickly he (and his dealer) could request backup from others. He assessed whether or not the dealer was "tooled up" and ready to fight back, if he was stoned or otherwise impaired, and how relaxed and unsuspecting he was. On other occasions, however, William assessed the viability and defensibility of 'ambush' robberies over time and repeated interactions (Wright and Decker, 1997a, p 98). By blending into the street world as a drug consumer, he established a co-presence then used short transactions to establish where drugs and cash were hidden and if the signs were that a dealer was "takeable". If William was physically more imposing than his victim, for example, then violence was available. If he felt he wanted the cash more than his dealer and was prepared to do whatever it took to get it, then a sudden switch in persona could provoke shock and demonstrate his own unpredictability. Once word got out about this, however, such behaviour burned William, and people stopped servicing him.

Our interviewees did not cheat everyone they encountered, only strangers or irregular buyers and sellers, people who were naïve and seemed unlikely to retaliate, or who were obnoxious and offensive and "deserved" to be mistreated. Interviewees often employed 'techniques of neutralization' (Sykes and Matza, 1957) to rationalize and justify violent "set-up buys", such as if the dealer was careless, annoying, unprofessional, "taking the piss", or waving his money around. For example:

I: *Yeah, what did you do? Did you grab it and run?*

William: Nah, man, run, fuck sake. Just said, 'Give me that.' Obv[iously] he was shocked, but fuck it. Got up in his face. He shat it and gave me the money. Took the pills as well … fuck it, I don't feel bad. He knew what he was getting into, don't he? His fault for no[t] protecting himself.

William indicates a lack of remorse and considers his behaviour as permissible on the grounds of an unofficial criminal code that his victim knew what he was getting into. It is not that William lacked self-control or demonstrated high impulsivity when presented with an easy opportunity to engage in crime, but rather he made a rational choice and worked any unofficial criminal codes to his advantage (Anderson, 1999; Mamayek et al, 2016).

Robbery may not always be as 'in your face' as the efforts shown by William that got him effectively blacklisted. Derek, who was a friend of participant Ronald, discusses a time in which he, as a drug dealer looking to get a good deal, went to the open market to procure drugs:

'My usual boy [drug dealer] was dry. Had literally fuck all over a few weeks, don't know that was going on cause he always had green [weed] and white [cocaine]. Still had my own punters to supply. If I didn't get up and running I would be out, outta business, goes fast if you're not on it. I wouldn't usually go to the [inter] net but needed green defo. Is my main source, know … [after putting up a post on social media] a boy gets back to me, giving me pure half cut prices, but only if I can get there that day, so didn't really have time to get prepped, know. I took wee Ronald wi' me for the ride. We turn up in the BM[W] and this [skinny] wee dude with a pure gammy leg is standing there on [X street].

Said who I was and gave him the money, he jumps into this house, well, a tenement, you know, the sandstone ones up [East End] way. Anyways he doesn't come out, so I text the wee fanny, "Fuck's keeping you?", and no reply. I ring him, and he said, "Fucking no getting your money, you know who so and so is, aye, well, that's my man. His house am in. Come to the door and you will be shot." That was that. I knew he wasn't talking shit but cause no going to just walks into a house and sit down and say, "Get to fuck and wi' that gangster" if you're no[t]. Especially when you're a gammy-legged bastard yourself. I called about obviously, and my mate from that wi' said aye, he [the contact seller] was friends with this gangster, and they always did that shit.'

As Derek notes, moving beyond his usual trusted contacts and using the internet to search for goods was always risky, a strategy he would usually avoid. However, he had his own customers to supply so he acted through fear of losing clientele and ventured into the open market. He was enticed in by the promise of cheap drugs, and because he only had until the end of the day to act, he did not have time to properly vet this contact and investigate whether or not this may be a scam. He moved too quickly and without due diligence.

Derek took Ronald along to the pickup location because Ronald was a known criminal with a violent reputation. Derek presumed this would be adequate backup and after seeing the seller had a disability and was willing to enter the house on Derek's behalf to collect the drugs, he felt confident enough to hand over his money. But this was all part of the illusion. The seller had lured them into a false sense of security because in reality he was working for what Pearson and Hobbs (2001) would refer to as a 'face', a known figure in the local criminal underworld, someone not to be messed with. Derek was duped and after several phone calls to confirm as much, he left without even chapping the doors in the tenement building. Robbery through deception and verbal threats made over the phone.

In the aforementioned situation, bringing Ronald to the drug deal was like bringing a knife to a gun fight. Another drug dealer, Alonso, described similar experiences where first encountering criminals higher up the food chain:

'I've never been robbed, like a guy robbing me at my face. People have bumped me, or usually they might try and intimate you, like saying, "I've not got your money, what you want me to do?" and it's like they are actually saying, "I do have it but I don't fear you enough to pay you," and that's the way it usually happens when people are trying to come at it, bump you, aye.'

Dealers robbed other dealers or potential customers robbed dealers in ways vast and inventive. The common denominator was often some form of lie or deception that gave the illusion of asymmetric power, such as when Derek thought his dealer had a physical disability. Essentially the robber plays possum to lure the dealer into his or her trap, gaining their trust and empowerment. William indicated that this was a common tactic used by those who would rob dealers, and told a story about an associate of his:

'One boy I knew would sell drugs to guys, like guys that weren't up to much, or he would ask them to store drugs for him and give them money, just like then and there, so they isn't turning it down. Then that night he would arrange for someone to break in and steal it or set it up so they got robbed just a wee while later after buying from him, and take the drugs back. It was fucking low, but he would do that again and again, selling this same kilo of coke. Just like roping them in. If it was a break-in he used [Mr White], but always [Chris] if a robbery, cause he is hefty aggressive, get me. That's his best [friend].'

William said that in this scenario, the experienced drug dealer, who was well known and had physical stature, would sell to independent dealers and then exploit their inexperience in the market. He would gain valuable personal information from them, such as their home address or where they stored drugs, then secretly arrange for them to be robbed. The experienced dealer would hire his best friend to carry out the robbery, or another individual he contracted with if a break-in or theft was required. If drugs were purchased 'on tick' (credit) and not paid for upfront he would then double-down on the scam by demanding interest from his victims when they inevitably missed payment deadlines or returned to purchase drugs from him again.

More often than not, dealers would be robbed by people they knew, or knew of, or had some connection to. Robbery was far from random. Yet, as William indicates earlier, theft and burglary were also utilized in an effort to cast doubt over who was responsible and insulate perpetrators from reprisals; to the extent that unsuspecting victims would come back for more. Reasonable suspicion and the benefit of the doubt were what kept cycles of revenge and retaliation alive. Alonso explained his own experience with this:

'Worst one is when I have been working wi' people and they rip you off and kid on they don't. *Wasn't them.* I was out on tag and had to go home obviously, you know cause the tag, it goes off if you're not in the house at a certain time. My mate, I was selling a wee bit of prop [pure cocaine], [he] knew this and waited till I got in, and then phones me up: "[The boss] is wanting their money." I was like, "Well, they need to wait till I can get out tomorrow." He is saying, "No, no, you need to get it now," pure putting pressure on me. I obviously can't get out the house, so said to him to come to mine and get the money. So, he turns up and starts again, "Aye, he is wanting a cut off the gear as well." Asking for half the gear back, so move to someone else. I thought it was bullshit. This guy knows I don't keep it here but keep it elsewhere at another house, but he just didn't know where. I tell him to get, but he is pure back at the door showing me calls from a private number and all that. I gave him the keys and said go and get it then. He then calls me from the [other property], "It's gone." … I fucking knew he took it and just stole it, can't prove it but. Worst thing, but he then says he wants his money for the bumped gear. Gets this other mad cunt to call me and trying to put pressure on me to give him my money for the gear he has just bumped off me. I told him to get to fuck, and he is saying [I] am getting done. Fuck it, I will slash him if I see him … nah, mate, I told that cunt to fuck off and stopped anything with him. His loss.'

Another interviewee, Addington, fell victim to an almost identical scheme whereby an associate of his emptied his stash house on the back of false allegations and a fabricated story:

'I was still on tag, you see … he called me up, "Mate, I have [known criminal] on the phone, giving me this and that, better get my money mate." I knew it was bullshit, looking back he was too desperate. I didn't want him having my number so took his word on it … [He went] to the [store house and] got it. Phoned me back, "Where the fuck is it, mate, you've been done. Someone has taken it. It is not here." Speaking all shaky. Like worried, as though he was worried.'

Unlike Alonso, however, Addington didn't let it go; he later robbed his friend back. His motivation was primarily to erase his own drug debt, but also to make right this earlier wrong and settle the score.

Concluding remarks

This chapter explored the dynamics of robbery, mostly at the retail end of the illicit drugs market. Some robbers work in groups to increase their chances of success, but even then, motivated offenders can underestimate the suitability of their targets, some of whom operate under the capable guardianship of more serious, organized criminals. Where dealers face more significant risks is at the lower tier of the market, especially when dealing in open markets. The point at which they are most vulnerable to confidence tricks and ambush attacks is during the exchange of money or product, or whenever they have to rely on a third party delivering the drugs, doing drop-offs on their behalf, or when couriering and collecting from a stash house.

FIVE

Trust No One

In the organized crime literature, it is often said that what keeps criminals 'organized' and together in the absence of courts and contracts is bonds of trust (von Lampe 2016). Trust reduces uncertainty regarding the behaviour of any partners in crime. However, the literature also shows that people who tend towards criminality are rarely 'reliable, trustworthy, or cooperative' (Gottfredson and Hirschi, 1990, p 213), and life in crime is fraught with uncertainty, distrust, suspicion verging on paranoia, and misunderstanding (Gambetta, 1993). This chapter examines some of this, including how robberies can occur from within gangs themselves. It also explores the progression from spontaneous robberies into planned robberies with a case study of participant Gee, who had transitioned from robbing members of the general public to robbing drug users and drug dealers – including his own friends. Gee explains how robbery was a viable way for him to move up the drug distribution ladder.

Robbing Peter to pay Paul

Smartphones and social media have led to the 'hybridization' of street offending – that is, crime that takes place on the street but is facilitated online, and vice versa (Roks et al, 2020). For example, there has been an increase in the phenomena of 'catfishing', whereby someone will create a fictional persona or fake identity to lure someone into a relationship online. This term is often used in the context of online dating, but our research found it applies to robbery as well. It was not uncommon for individuals to 'put out lines' on the internet, meaning tempting classified ads and bargain deals, and wait for unsuspecting individuals to reply. As a youth, Gee and his friend would engage in petty theft and robbery, sometimes with their peers in tow. Robbery began opportunistically with the duo simply taking advantage of situations that made people vulnerable to crime. After experiencing the thrills and the economic gains of robbery, however, Gee and his colleague set up a more organized system whereby they would play catfish to pull in their victims. Gee explains the process:

'Me and [Individual C] would put up ads on Gumtree ... things that [boys our age at that time] would have [liked]. [Computer] games, slasher caps, mind them? Some things we never had but advertised anyway ... like [jewellery] ... [we gave a] fake address ... [we wore] Berghaus jackets ... They are good for pulling the hood up and hiding blades, [be]cause you had the inside zip pockets ... when [the buyer] showed, we jumped out and robbed them. I wasn't into robbing women, but [my friend] did a few times ... [we would] put a knife to their throat. I always went behind them and put knife to their side but [my friend] held it to their throat ... meant they couldn't run, and didn't know where I was standing exactly, [so] they were [unable] to react ... only took money, rings, [that] stuff. No point in taking credit cards or motor keys ... [did] that for about two years, until I got caught ... never got caught doing the crime ... [but] when I [traded] the [stolen goods] into the shop, they changed [policy], and you needed to give ID ... When we got caught, robberies around the area probably stopped [laughs].'

By engaging in opportunistic street robbery first, Gee gained the requisite experience and expertise to level up in the robbery game. Robbery is a progressive art, and as such, Gee's early forays into robbery gave him the confidence to begin targeting "bigger jobs". Seldom does an individual engage in such orchestrated crime without building up some experience first. After Gee was imprisoned for trading stolen goods, he honed his craft further to target drug dealers and users specifically. Gee still put ads on social media to lure his targets, only this time he was touting drugs, not consumer goods:

'I was more dealing, starting to deal like proper, drugs, aye, round that time [when released from prison], a [contact] gives white [cocaine] for myself to shift, eccies [ecstasy pills] as well … [robbery is] fast. You wouldn't think so, it is addictive. You think of everything like, if I earn this and spend that, then if I am doing robberies on the side, then it could be more profit. It is greed really. It is as if you're thinking, I need to get cash to get a set-up to start out, but easier to steal someone else's than [building my own over time]. Spend their money, sell their drugs … [My friend] didn't get [incarcerated] and was still doing [robberies]. He had hooked up wi' another young boy [Jiro] from the scheme. Think I was, hmm, must have been 20, 21, say. People were [at the time] using BBM [BlackBerry Messenger], know. It is Snapchat now. No[t] then. Put out a shout: "I've this much white, this much green [weed], brown [heroin],", it's all bullshit anyway. Same routine really … were stealing money from [end-users]. Was a bit different, guys were older, and would usually come with a pal or two in the car, so we would have to give an address in middle of fucking nowhere, like parks, [football] pitches.'

Gee explained that once he began targeting drug dealers and users, the likelihood of legal consequences diminished but extra-legal blowback was a perennial risk, so his planning became more and more elaborate:

'[We would acquire] a stoler [stolen vehicle] and take it to the place … [we would] have our actual [car] parked up close by. So they can't track the car, know what I am saying, mate? You have to always change it up constantly. We didn't buy the stoler's from legits, or steal them. You get one of the young mob to do that, like only a couple of hours beforehand so need to know people in the loop, ready to go [clicking fingers again and again] … [we] would be in the driver's seat in the car, parked up in the place, well before anyone got there. [I would] still smudge the reg[istration] plate, [and would] sit in the car … Wee Jiro would be out in the bushes. The parks were always pitch black so hardly able to see.'

The robberies themselves also became more violent:

'Would wait till they arrived, but no make a move so they would be parked opposite and it is just us, so they would text or call the number we had gave. Asking, "That you in car?" I'd be like, "Drive up to the driver window." We would get them to drive up so the car is side by side, like to talk, and that, know. You always talk for a wee bit, chit-chat, know. Sitting in the car, I would ask to see the money, and if they handed it over, that was it … My mate would pull out the old Browning pistol, know. It was real, aye … [My friend] would stick it in his face, "Don't fucking move"… Wee Jiro would run out, pan the back window with a brick. They always took off. If not, he would stab a tyre and get in our [car], and we would be off. Some cunts didn't hand the money but, so I would point to a bag we planted over at bushes whatever and say, "The gear is in there." Gave some stories about, planted it case they were cops. Meant one had to get out, or if it was the driver, then he would kill the engine. Was always close enough they would [not] drive over. Soon as that door opened but, "Got you, you prick," meant the locks were off. Jiro would bolt over and pull a shooter. His was an old shotgun. It never worked, and never had bullets anyways [but it] looks fucking terrifying when up at your chest. He is a mad bastard … Most times, cause everyone was sitting and you have a gun, so they shite it and freeze, you know. Demand the money. Only the money, especially after I got caught before [trading items into pawn stores]. Need to lie low but for a bit, cause some boys would be trolling the net looking for you. After a bit [we had to] get others to put shout outs [because we couldn't] keep using the same shout on[line]. Sometimes it went tits up and we would have to bail … It is dodgy [but gives] a buzz, a heavy one.'

Gee would target only those who had significant money, offering deals for larger quantities of drugs, in order to make the effort worth it. The success of the robbery was largely based on Gee's ability to control as many variables as possible, practising and planning the event, anticipating potential moves and what could go wrong. While this method was suited for a time, as Gee notes, some victims would seek to come after Gee and his friends and thus, eventually they had to change tactic again. However, the key to success, said Gee, was getting his hands on the money first, then executing the perfect ambush. As the robberies became more complex, he needed a team to make them work and eventually the group progressed from robbing retail-level dealers to wholesalers.

While Gee and his gang robbed their own 'customers', the incentives for buying big and completing high-end drug deals meant that the people they enticed with their schemes were typically other drug dealers, or at least social suppliers with considerable financial disposal, looking to purchase privately before consuming recreationally with peers and colleagues (for discussion see McPhee et al, 2019). Gee and his colleagues realized that if they could retain the drugs they displayed as being for sale, even steal other drugs in addition to this, they could supplement the robbery gig with a more stable form of income – drug dealing. In fact, during the research we learned that dealers would at times target other dealers for robbery, less to resell in a one-off transaction and more to gain the money and drugs necessary to "start up" their own illegal business ventures.

I thought we were mates? Intra-gang robbery

In a world where trust is fragile, some interviewees only really trusted immediate family. Twin brothers Mc-C and Mc-D, for example, went into business together robbing drug dealers in an effort to finance their own drug distribution venture:

Mc-C: The only guy I ever get involved with is my brother, course.

Mc-D: Done everything together, it has always been that. Know, start school same time, same mates, and college, lassies and what, know.

Mc-C: Same age as one another, suppose it is likely that with most twins. Most brothers even.

I: *I see. So how did you both start out? Did one influence the other, or both decide on dealing?*

Mc-C: Nah, wasn't that one way doing this and the other that. It was more the thing we had been brought up in, in the house. Our family house.

Mc-D: Know, it is like, we were raised.

Mc-C: Aye, well, no, not really. We were, sold speed and ecstasy for our dad. But we stopped that, in our late teenage period, like 18. I met [my girlfriend, Kerry], and [Mc-D] her pal. I was more serious, than him. But kind of stopped any trouble, bad behaviour, then went back to it.

I: *Went back to dealing or crime in general?*

Mc-C: Yeah, like more professional … I split wi' Kerry and he [Mc-D] had still been fucking about wi' her mate. We actually fell out over money issues, like we never had enough [laughs]. [Decided]

I wasn't going to be like that struggling wi' again. Lassies just don't respect that.

Mc-D: I had [been selling drugs] with [James]. Mc-C wanted a piece. He was like always the smart one.

Mc-C: No that smart ... I got a hold of a shotgun ... It had been my auld man's stepsister's man's, if that's right. Like my aunt. Step aunt. It had been her man's, well, ex-man's. Confusing anno ... I had the shotgun. Mc-D an auld machete, and we, eh, went through to James' sister's house and asked to wait on James.

Mc-D: Well, I pretended as though I hadn't seen him [James], know, to get in, know.

Mc-C: Aye, it was quite shitty. He grabbed her and flung her down and booted her, no hard but you've glanced her, aye. Aye, she's a big lass, and can handle herself, so just to quieten her, stop her from acting out at us, she's gubby as fuck ... Mc-D called James, 'We are here and you've ten minutes to get her with five grand, and the kilo he had been keeping.'

I: *Seems quite short to get that. How you know he wouldn't be coming after you's raging?*

Mc-C: You don't. He might be, but end of, we have his sister and had threatened to take a digit off every five mins he was late. So, like, no time to think ... I was only wanting to get on the go, get me, it's the start-up, I am in my [age], I've no time to be buying and selling and working to get to where I want. It's, it's, like bang bang here, now.

This statement from the twins Mc-C and Mc-D demonstrates that even among colleagues, in the drugs game there is often little trust at all. Mc-D had been selling relatively low quantities of cocaine, alongside a range of prescription medication and amphetamines. James was the main dealer, operating at wholesale level, largely on an individual basis and using Mc-D whom he had met through his partner at the time, to sell smaller quantities on the side and to make wider contacts.

Things changed when Mc-C "split" from his then partner, Kerry. Kerry left in part because Mc-C had no money. She was rumored to be dating a known drug dealer in the area with significant means and Mc-C thought he might win her back if he changed his financial situation. Mc-C already had some criminal connections and approached his brother Mc-D and the pair decided to go into business together. Blood is thicker than water. Mc-D turned on his friend James because James was an easy target. Mc-D knew where he kept his money and drugs and this meant James could quickly be "turned over". There would also be little repercussions because the brothers had a numerical advantage over James and a greater degree of criminal capital to threaten him with, leveraging their family reputation and criminal histories. Not to mention they had a gun. By targeting James' sister and threatening to sever her fingers, Mc-C was telegraphing his ruthlessness. The brothers used the proceeds of this crime to start up and get ahead in the drugs game and give them a footing:

> **Mc-C**: The [resources] from that [event], did help, aye. We blew about 1,200 straight away, just going out, stuff, like I pure needed a new jacket. We put the rest out [to work], and aye, we got a decent sum in from the sale[s]. You get it in tick, a loan upfront, so that and having the cash for a deposit for more, more coke, means I can get more.

> **Mc-D**: Cause you have already put the down payment down.

> **Mc-C**: It is, yeah, it's credit, isn't it, good credit. A bank gives you a bigger mortgage, don't they, wi' more deposit. Same idea.

I: *Did you find doing James over meant sellers might find you both too dodgy to work with? Because of the James incident?*

Mc-C: Eh, nah, no really. No, I don't think so. No. Scott, the boy James was buying his gear from. It isn't like he sells to James so James works for him. That would be like Mc-D sold for James so he worked for James, but no really cause he always paid James up front for the gear to sell, or same, wi' a deposit, know. So, cause we were buying from Scott doesn't mean we work for him. James didn't work for Scott. He [Scott] happened to have gear to sell, we had cash to buy. James didn't. He still had to move it. We bought it.

I: *Did you think about robbing Scott though? If you had…*

Mc-C: No, fuck sake, Scott is my dad's mate. Com' on [laughs]. Not going to do that … [I would have] went to Scott before. I knew Scott before James. Still need the mula [money], but, know. He is into business. It's not you give to mate cause they're mates. Need hard money to pay.

The money and drugs from the armed robbery of James enabled the brothers to put down a larger deposit on the purchase of drugs, meaning that more could be gained on "tick" or credit, to be paid back at a later date. The brothers purchased drugs from their dad's friend, Scott, who was in prison at the time of this interview. Scott was someone well known to the brothers but they tried to keep their personal relationship and business relationship separate, even if boundaries became blurry at times. Given what Mc-D did to James, it was unclear whether it was really friendship that prevented the brothers from robbing Scott or fear of the consequences. It also turned out that Scott and the brothers had sourced their firearm from the same person, which would have made things complicated had one then used it against the other.

The brothers argued they did not see themselves as 'robbers', it certainly wasn't their master identity, although they certainly engaged in robbery:

> **Mc-C**: I wouldn't see myself, or us, me and him, as drug dealer[s], or robbers. You do what you do to get by, that's what I would say. I am a drug dealer, aye, if you say that, aye. I suppose, I am. I am not a thief, or a backstabber.
>
> **I**: *What about the other acts of robbery though?*
>
> **Mc-C**: It wasn't robbery, like I robbed them. I don't feel great about it. See it like this, you a thief?
>
> **I**: *No, I wouldn't say I am.*
>
> **Mc-C**: You stole but? Like anytime.
>
> **I**: *Yeah, course, I have stolen. In school we would steal Rolos from Mack Snack.*
>
> **Mc-C**: Exactly, but you don't say, 'I am a thief', a stealer. You did it, but you ain't it. Same wi' us.

Mc-C and Mc-D defaulted on a payment once and fell into debt with their main supplier after police seized their stash. The brothers tried to find another supplier fast because they had customers to serve, but word got out about their debt and the brothers were compelled to pay it off before others would do business with them. To do this, they turned to a rather unconventional form of robbery – robbing themselves:

> **Mc-C**: [I had drug debts], sometimes payments are missed. That happens. It's life. I know Scott isn't coming after me, us, I mean. He is all right. But he isn't going to give more. I was thinking about not paying it, [approximately £15,000], it['s] not a drop, know.

Mc-D: Scott don't know, but we did try [Ralph], Scott's pal. He wasn't up for that but.

Mc-C: Yeah, sure, we asked. Wasn't serious but. It was like, 'Would you'… [Ralph] would never do that. We wouldn't. Word gets about it you are [faulting on] debts … [we robbed] Steph. I feel like…

Mc-D: Crap.

Mc-C: Aye, crap. Like crap. Steph [would hold cocaine] for us. So like it's robbing from us, ourselves. It becomes his debt, and that gets us money. He had a savings account that we deposited in, so he got that every few month, so I knew there was money … [we simply] withheld [the payment].

Mc-D: We did let him off wi' some of [the debt money], but you know.

As the brothers explain, they robbed their own stockpile of cocaine and then moved their debt on to the associate tasked with overseeing it by withholding his quarterly payments, proving once again that in the criminal underworld, you really should trust no one.

In their study of gang-related homicides, Decker and Curry (2002) found that most gang homicides were in fact not carried out between gangs but within gangs. This carries over to the crime of robbery, we found, to the extent that our participants reported being robbed more frequently by members of their own gang than by members of rival gangs. The following case study demonstrates this point, where Calvin, a leading member of a young street gang held hostage and robbed a fellow gang member, Sam, in what was a long and sustained attack. It is important to establish their social status during this period. First, Calvin:

'I had been boxing for years, mind [remember] the YMCA in Paisley, aye. I first went there no that long after I went to high school. Must have been about 13, I think. My mum was worried about me getting bullied in school [be]cause I was wee. I loved the boxing. Was when I was at my best, best version of myself, know. No one really thought I was like a top boy in the year, in first year [of secondary school]. It was more [names]. I knew Gary and Baz from primary so was sound wi' them both, and me and Frank hit it off right away in [secondary school]. We sat together in maths and was a laugh … [Keegan, however, I] didn't know him cause he [went to different primary school]. Was a big cunt, like a massive cunt, know. I first seen him I actually thought he was a man, no even kidding you on … We got into an argument in English, him acting the cunt and all. Just being a bully to a wee boy we kicked around wi'. I told him to give it a bye and he started on me. I said nothing. Just said I would meet him after school. He was giving it big: "Look at me, am the big man." Saying this and whatever. I knew I could fight but … I walked up the big path along the front of the school. Mind, everyone following me saying, "You actually going to fight him?", "He's a tank," usual pish. I clocked him coming down the hill and just walked up and launched my school bag on the ground. He came swaggering down and I literally just gave him a straight right to the nose and it burst. He might have had fights before, but I could tell he hadn't actually been involved in a scrap. I had from the boxing. He put his head down and tried to grab me with one arm and choke me with the other. Pure fucking idiot, rendering both his arms out the fight right away. I just gave him three rapid [punches] around the chin and he decked it. I didn't kick him, no[t] me. I prefer my hand. Said, "Get up," and waited then just leathered him again with another few punches. Did the same again, and again. Till he tried to run, but he was fucked from getting punched about so I just chased him and battered him again. Did that for about half an hour till he made it to his door. A couple of birds [females] were, no joke, greeting because the beating he was getting ... Everyone [after that] said, "Calvin's top cunt."'

With one very public display of violence, Calvin rose to become a 'top boy' in his school year. Afterwards, he become popular and began to socialize with known gang members in the area who were a year or two older than him. Before long, he was an established gang member.

Sam's rise through the social hierarchy of secondary school was quite different:

'I would have said I was [a] quiet guy growing up, [but] nobody else seems to think so [laughs]. I have always been like a guy that finds things funny. Like, say, for example, I like SpongeBob Square Pants. I know, I know, it's for little children. I love it. Absolutely kill myself laughing. Same with, you ever watch *Johnny Bravo*? What a show, "Huh u huh u" [karate noises and gestures]. What a show. I was more into having giggles, getting on, than fighting. I could get on well with people. Was able to connect well ... [In secondary school] my best mates were Frank and Joe ... [we] met in school, through sitting next to one another in a few classes. You meet people, don't you? Weekends everyone would go out drinking, hang out. The Young Team hung around the swing park. Frank was my mate so he had my back. He was a main figure on the scene and I was his best mate. Made me a part of the squad ... I got into selling [weed], some pills on the odd time ... I wouldn't like say I myself am a drug dealer, or at the time I did it. I know other people would say, "Sam is a drug dealer." I did good well, but it wasn't like who I seen myself to be ... I do think my personality, being mates with Frank, and [selling drugs] likely made me a popular figure on the place.'

So, Calvin joined the local street gang because he was a fighter. Sam joined because he was friends with the fighters and owing to his outgoing personality, he landed a gig as a minor drug dealer. How they entered the gang and the skills they brought to it afforded them different levels of status among local youths. Calvin was seen as the alpha male, whereas Sam was a bit of a joker. He could "not fight his way out of a wet paper bag", he said. Sam relied on Frank for protection, but protection was not always guaranteed because Frank wasn't working with Sam in the drugs business:

> 'Yeah, most guys likely gave me a bit more leeway because [of my friendship with Frank]. We weren't selling [drugs] together. Was not like that at all. He had nothing to do with that. He is actually right against drugs, of any sorts. He drinks, a lot [laughs]. Gets himself into more trouble because he drinks, but for some reason, drugs are off the table ... [Gary's] cousin was selling nine bars to my cousin, and when I seen him he would sell a bit to myself ... I don't meet my cousin much beyond that. He had a wife, they didn't stay in the town any more. She moved away. He went as well.'

Although Sam was able to procure drugs, and while this was through kinship, his cousin was much older (in his 30s) and while he dealt drugs at retail level, this was primarily to supplement his low wages from a full-time job as a laborer. Sam mentions his supplier "doesn't get involved in beef [trouble]". This is because he is married, has a job, and other responsibilities such as "a house" and "three little children". Such responsibilities means that Sam's elder cousin refrains from getting into any affairs that are not his own, and while being "a bit of a Jack the Lad ... up to a lot of trouble" he has outgrown gang life and is settled, with "too much to lose".

Most people who go on to become successful drug dealers in their adult years tend to have criminal reputations and the ability to 'handle themselves' and/or have established criminal connections and support (McLean, 2019). These resources help them avoid victimization, or if not avoid it, then at least retaliate against it. By selling drugs, Sam had entered into a 'high risk' and overly 'masculine' environment (Hutton, 2005), yet was in a precarious position even though he was a member of a gang because his main gang contact, Frank, was not his business partner, and Frank's status as the gang's top boy was under pressure from Calvin:

> 'Me and Frank got on, but weren't pal, pals, know, weren't pure pals, you know. He was the top yain from his bit [of the town]. People all said I was, or me and Gary maybe, from our end. I would batter Gary, well, I did batter him once, but he's a heavy blade man, and slashed me in the fight across the ear and back of my neck … [I wasn't] scared of Frank. He definitely wasn't scared of me. More like we respected each other. Aye, I am wary. No doubt he was. I could tell he was. See it in the eyes, you know.'

There was an uneasy peace between Calvin and Frank, a mutual respect that meant they were hesitant to fight one another to establish who was really top dog. Still, if Calvin ever fought Frank and won, he would cement his position as leader of the gang.

Sam had no doubt Calvin wanted to be the undisputed top boy, but rather than fight Frank, he instead tried to intimidate Sam in Frank's presence, to provoke a response and undermine his status. Calvin first tried not paying Sam for 20 Valium pills he had supplied him with. A week later, Calvin asked Sam for 100 more pills, around £80 worth of product:

> 'I knew he was going to ask for them [the pills]. He had only paid me [the first time] after a song and dance about it a few days earlier. I had said I had none, but

he knew that was a lie since I was still giving my other friends them. We were out at the shops, the main shops at the town centre. I was in getting a mixer for my Friday night drinking session and I bumped into him. He was steaming. The usual from Calvin at the weekend. He asked again. I couldn't say, "Oh, I don't have any," since I had literally sold about 30 to the lads he was in company with. I agreed and went behind the shop, round the back of it to give him them.'

However, the pills were not all Calvin was after:

'Next thing, he grabs me by the neck and takes the lot. Course I thought it was over. Yeah, I was crapping myself, he is little but he is a brawler of a lad. He then put his hand in my pocket and took out my wallet. Actually emptied it before my eyes, and hit me with the empty wallet. I was looking at my friend James, and the lad he was with, like, "Come on, guys, help me out here." To be fair, James did try and say something but got a slap over the face for his trouble. He started slapping me because I only had 150 in my wallet. Said we were going to the bank for another 50. I wasn't happy but agreed to get him to fuck. I did think about shouting to people when walking round, like to adults, I was only about 16 so was a little lad [but] I was too much a coward. Couldn't get it out my mouth. People must have seen but, I was crying, not pure crying but sobbing, with shock more than anything, wi' him like a bear behind me shoving me. I put the number and card in the machine, and he pushes me out the way and lifts 250 out. I was really angry. Thought that was it, but he then took me to my house, and had me go in. I only stayed with my gran and didn't want her to worry. We went into my house and he took the box from under the bed with not kidding around 700, maybe 800 pills, a thousand in money, and all my [weed]. Marched me down the woods, and got wasted, then after midnight, well hours after midnight marched me back to the bank and took another 250 out my bank.'

The robbery lasted over ten hours.

Calvin avoided any confrontation with Frank by apologizing to Sam and offering to return the goods taken, blaming his behaviour on intoxication. But Calvin never actually returned any more than £20 to Sam, and although Sam felt the apology was empty, he had no further recourse because Frank wanted to avoid a fight with Calvin at all costs.

We heard similar stories about intra-gang robbery, although none quite as egregious as this. Because not all gang members dealt drugs, those who did were vulnerable to an 'inside job', especially if they lacked the ability to defend themselves, because they had money and product. This type of robbery, although opportunistic, was very much based upon established relationships and power dynamics within the gang, and typically followed a brief build-up of tension or an internal gang struggle where boundaries were being tested to see how far someone could be pushed. Gang members would give people humiliating orders, challenge them to fight, verbally abuse them, or help themselves to goods already in their possession, to test the waters of a full-scale attack. Contrary to popular belief, the gang in this context is less a source of protection and more a source of victimization. Interestingly, however, as with Calvin and Sam, intra-gang robberies rarely involved a weapon, or even actual bodily harm. Instead, it was psychological intimidation and bullying. Some individuals reported being routinely victimized with their assailant moving between periods of befriending them and robbing them, making the relationship complex.

Later in the interview, Calvin tried to justify robbing Sam by noting that the occupation of a drug dealer was someone who sold misery. This was a common excuse, as noted earlier in Chapter Two. However, Sam was really a social supplier who dealt mostly to his young peers, so just how much misery he inflicted upon the community is questionable:

> 'I liked Sam. He was all right. To be honest, he was just one of the guys on the [periphery], not really that important, that makes sense, mate? Me, Frank, Gary, were top ones about the place so you only really care about other top ones, not wee goobers like Sam … Aye, suppose it did, it felt powerful, you know. I could get him to do whatever I wanted. I wasn't a dick about it. I was all right, speaking away. Told him I just wanted what he had. He sold drugs, mate, was a scumbag. Deserved to be robbed. Made money off other people's misery. Was a smirking wee prick anyway.'

Calvin continued to victimize his own gang members and later he progressed to robbing other drug dealers and occasionally members of the public, at knifepoint.

Sam noted how the robbery really exposed his lowly status in the gang and how he was made to feel "powerless" within his own social circle. Sam was robbed not only of his drugs and money, but also his dignity:

> 'Wasn't nice, no. You kind of feel powerless. Calvin is just a bully, always has been a bully. How did I feel? He was just taking advantage of me. He was a brute of a lad. A boxer and all. I was a wee skinny thing, never had a fight in my life. He was acting like we were all okay, but he made me sit in the woods until the next morning. My gran worried, no one heard from me. He abused his name [reputation]. I always had nice stuff, he was a jealous bastard. You think he would have done that had Frank been there, or tried it with Gary. He sold Valium. He never tried to rob him. A liberty taker. Frank let me down as well but.'

Sam learned from this experience and began paying Frank for his protection, effectively bringing him into his drugs business.

Concluding remarks

Gang members regularly cite protection and safety as motivations for joining gangs (Densley 2018), the idea being that affiliating with a gang could thwart attempts of intimidation, robbery, theft, or violence, especially in dangerous neighbourhoods. However, this chapter demonstrates – in line with prior studies – that this must be contrasted against group processes in gangs that elevate risk of violence (Short and Strodtbeck, 1965; Decker, 1996), as well as the fact that offenders and victims are often one and the same. Risky lifestyles, routine activities, and individual propensities for crime create non-randomness in victimization (for a review, see Turanovic and Pratt 2019). In the end, some of the worst robberies we learned about in the course of our research came from within not outside of the gang.

SIX

Life After Robbery

"That's the guy," Ricky said. "Couldn't forget his face even if I tried."

"That's good, son, now try and see if you recognize his accomplice from the next set," the officer replied as he drew out a second booklet of faces.

It had been several months since the robbery and Ricky was down at the police station to relive it all again. He was happy the police were at least following up and doing their job, although Ricky would have preferred street justice over legal justice. He had been taught as a youth to seek out as soon as possible anyone who threatened, bullied, or harassed him, otherwise fear would grow and become all-consuming. He could feel that fear setting in. Part of Ricky was eager to see his assailants again to enact revenge and possibly get back the 600 quid taken from him, but another part of him was afraid they would re-victimize him if he ever bumped into them again.

After flipping through the multiple pages of faces, some offenders, some not, Ricky suddenly stopped at the page with a photo of the tattoo guy, the man who literally had gone for Ricky's jugular vein during their brief encounter on the streets.

"That's the guy there. His wee pal with the blade," Ricky said, pointing to the page.

"That's fine. Thank you for coming in," the officer said. "We will take it from here and will be in touch." They stood up from the table.

"Can I ask their names before I go?" Ricky asked, optimistically. "I know that was them that I identified in the booklets."

"I can't disclose that information. But I can tell you that we have several witnesses who are willing to testify, who like yourself have been robbed or assaulted by these two," the officer stated.

A few weeks later, Ricky received a letter in the mail to attend court in the case against his two attackers, Stephen and Jimmy. At the trial, he came face-to-face with his assailants. Neither of them had made bail following their arrest so they were brought up from the holding cells below the courtroom. Stephen was the tall one and he cockily grinned as he stood there before the sheriff in handcuffs. Jimmy, on the other hand, was looking anxiously down at the ground. Neither looked over at Ricky, who never even took the stand because the attackers changed their plea to guilty right there in an effort to reduce the potentially long, but definite, prison sentence which would be handed down to them.

It emerged at the trial that Stephen and Jimmy were both heroin addicts. Stephen had a long rap sheet and lived with his mother. Jimmy had only one prior offence and lived with his girlfriend, who was also a heroin addict. The two men were charged with a six-week robbery spree, which began with the assault and battery of an elderly women who put up a fight after Stephen tried to wrestle her purse away from her on the street. She spent several weeks in hospital.

Two attacks in one day followed. A young boy on his way home from school was robbed at knifepoint and a few hours later, a drug dealer was stabbed during a robbery at his home. Next, the two men assaulted an elderly man on his doorstep after he asked the men to stop loitering there. They broke several of his ribs, strangled him with a cord, and stabbed him in the back as he lay prone on the ground. They also took the small change he had in his pocket.

Ricky's attack was next. The main evidence in Ricky's case was CCTV footage from the bank. As Ricky withdrew £600 from the teller, Stephen and Jimmy were watching, faces pressed against the glass door.

A break-in at the home of a drug dealer followed. The pair went in searching for money and drugs, but someone inside identified them from a prior contact, and the pair were subsequently arrested. There were likely many more robberies but that was all the police could pin on the pair. Still, it was enough to put them away for a few years. And so, Ricky had some closure. He put his robbery ordeal behind him, and moved on.

Three years later, Ricky was walking down the street, not far from where he had been robbed before. He glanced over his shoulder and into the sea of people out walking in the sunshine and caught a glimpse of a face. A familiar face. It was him. Stephen.

Ricky felt a horrible rush come over him, a strange sensation almost like he needed to go to the toilet. A series of thoughts travelled through his mind. Should he turn around and walk the other way, or slow down and hope Stephen didn't see him? Ricky was about to head into the nearest shop to buy himself some time when a different thought crept into his head.

"Fuck this. I'm not letting this wee prick run my life."

Three years on and Ricky was still embarrassed that he had been assaulted and robbed. He still felt emasculated by it and was still a little wary about walking through the backstreets. Suddenly, Ricky felt himself sliding back into an "old mode" of thinking and reacting, a past that he thought he had left behind.

You see, as a teenager Ricky had been involved in gangs and street fighting. He had even robbed people. For a while, he robbed drug dealers routinely. After his mum died, he did it to provide for his family, he tells us. Ricky initially was dealing drugs, but the lifestyle didn't really agree with him so instead he used his "inside knowledge" of the business to start picking off local drugs retailers and social suppliers. He said that he was so numb from the pain of losing his parent at the time that during a series of ambush robberies, he projected the air of someone extremely dangerous and not to be messed with.

Thinking back on that life now, however, Ricky feels a lot of guilt about how he treated others, and the heartache he knows he caused the families and friends of his victims. He cringes at the thought of some of the nasty things he did and we sense some self-loathing there, hatred even. But growing up in Glasgow, Ricky has learned to switch off his emotions on cue. He was come to grips with the fact that men fight because that's what men do. Men fight to exert control over the situation. Violence is a tool.

At that moment, with Stephen in front of him, Ricky remembered the buzz of it all, the thrill of not having to be scared any more. Ambush was best, the element of surprise, Ricky decided. He was finally going to have his revenge.

Ricky crossed the road, his eyes so fixed on his target that he was almost hit by a passing car. He then ducked down behind a parked car as Stephen approached, completely unaware of what was coming.

The crowd parted and suddenly Stephen moved in a way that implied he knew something was up. Our interviewees talked about this feeling a lot. A "Spidey sense" or "gut feeling" that something bad was about to happen but they were powerless to stop it. Stephen spun around, dipping his shoulder to glance behind him, only to receive Ricky's sweet right hook clean to his face. It was what they call in West Scotland 'a belter'. Stephen's head went spinning and he crashed down against the parked car. Ricky followed up with another blow but Stephen was already out cold.

A few seconds later, Stephen came to, and tried to get up, his eyes still dazed. "Fuck's that aboot?" he screamed.

Ricky wrapped his hands around Stephen's neck and choked him. Hard. Seconds ticked by, until a bystander said, "I think his eyes are going to pop. Let him go."

Ricky didn't let go. At that moment he felt he was going to choke Stephen to death. Until—

A burly hand on Ricky's shoulder pulled him off.

"Enough, come on, he has had enough," the voice beckoned.

Ricky let go. In front of him stood two police officers.

"What's this about, eh?" one of the officers inquired.

"Sorry, officers," Ricky said and immediately took a submissive position. He quickly explained the whole story. The officers ran a criminal record check to verify the story.

After a few minutes, the officers decided there was "nothing to see here" and moved everyone along. For even the police agreed that street justice was necessary in this case.

That was the last time Ricky got in a fight or was involved in crime. He says finding God was what turned his life around. Ricky is certainly not the first ex-gang member to sing the praises of religion for helping to turn his life around (for example Brenneman, 2011; Flores, 2013; Johnson and Densley, 2018; Bolden, 2020). Back when Ricky was robbing drug dealers for sport, he had convinced himself: "I am dammed and that is that. Accept it," but one day he picked up the phone and called the local Salvation Army and asked when their church service was. The internet wasn't the same back then, in fact he didn't even have it, so he just got the number from the Yellow Pages phone book. When he showed up at church, he felt he was doing what he was meant to be doing. But he was worried what others might think if he told them he was going to church or that he felt a calling from God. So, he continued acting bad, then at night when he was alone, he would pray and beg for forgiveness. Only after he moved out to a new house, away from some bad influences and his worst impulses, did Ricky start going to church consistently and feel confident enough to tell others that he was a practising Christian. He got baptized and it felt right.

Ricky still got pulled back into crime on occasion. He had friends and brothers and cousins who wanted "backup" and would get his involved "in their shite". He got into fights during Saturday morning amateur football league games or when he'd had too much to drink at the pubs and clubs. The precariousness of desistance from crime is a consistent theme in criminology (Veysey et al, 2013; Densley and Pyrooz 2019) and was something we heard from others too, like Gavin. We met Gavin earlier in the book – he had spent most of his adult life in and out of prison:

> 'The thing that the police do not understand is that when they say don't get into trouble any more, I still have to live in the place and the guys that caused the trouble are going to still come after me. They want me getting in trouble. If I run away it only makes them get wilder and want to get me even more because they think I am scared. They tell people and they are all thinking I am scared, but I am just wanting to stay out of trouble. You can't get away from the trouble and the police do not care. This has been the thing that makes it hard to get away from crime. I don't rob any more but because I after one time me and Ricky robbed one of the boys that had been saying loads of stuff to people and we caught him on the way to the shops and he got slashed with a broken bottle. I got a long time in jail for that because I had other stuff. Inside I got all these mental health assessments and they gave me case workers who said I had suffered PTSD [Post Traumatic Stress Disorder] and was actually insane [mentally ill] or something, and they helped me get a move away from the place I stayed before. I had been saying get me out of the place for years and the police will see that I stop getting into trouble, but they didn't and surprise, surprise, I got in trouble. Since I have been out, I have not got into any more trouble. The church stuff helps and keeps me from getting raging [and because I now] don't stay in the same place I don't have to deal with the people I had been fighting with coming after me as soon as I get out jail.'

Ricky agreed that desistence was not an end state, but rather an ongoing process. Even today he feels he might be one argument away from a homicide because crime has become part of who he is. But becoming a Christian has created a sense of control and a sense of humility, because he now puts others first, not himself. He can see how his actions affect others. And he puts God first and foremost.

One of the ways in which Ricky started putting others first was to help out his old friend, Gavin. Gavin explained:

'We started trying to help each other and stop getting into trouble. This older guy called Alan that Ricky knew would come round from a church out in Lanarkshire. I don't think Ricky went to that church ever but met him at some café for people that are trying to stop getting into trouble. The guy would talk over stuff to do with the Bible and that did help … Ricky and me would really talk about the Bible as in a way that was studying it. We would talk about God and what God was like and if he cared about us. Ricky said, "Yeah, I think so," but sometimes I would disagree over certain points. We would really [encourage one another] by just being mates and when the other person was going to do something daft, the other one would say don't do that. That was really it. The difference was that we cared for each other and that was probably the thing that helped the most. It was having a religion that we both could talk about and think the same on, and also having each other as mates, and caring for each other as mates helped. That was the things that helped.'

Life events known as 'turning points' are key to understanding the larger life course because they redirect us in significant ways (Elder, 1994). Family (parenthood) and legal work are key turning points in the lives of offenders (Laub and Sampson, 1993; Carlsson, 2012; Gundur, 2020), but religion was a consistent theme in the desistance narratives of our interviewees. For example, Jessie said:

'Before I started practising [spirituality] … I was my own god. I would say what was right and what was wrong …

That was my moral compass ... That's why I kept fucking up, cause I'm just a man, just flesh. You don't think that way beforehand ... When I became a servant of God, I realized His morality was right, always is. I was nothing ... I can see that now ... Living my life around the moral principle He puts in me guides me to live right [nowadays].'

Religious worship was often a venue for deep connection with others, creating opportunities for ex-offenders to intimately share their feelings and establish meaningful relationships away from criminal activity. Ex-offender Chris-O, described himself as a 'born-again':

'I never had a, like what you say, a moment of pure clarity or nothing like that, mate. More like I was getting fed up of the lifestyle, eh. Just waking up feeling pure shit in myself, and shit for the things I was getting up to, mate. After a while it gets pure [tiresome] ... I had been kind of drifting away from it all for a while if [I] am being honest ... Cause I'm not involved in what's going on, my [criminal companions] stopped asking me to do this or that. No going to lie, I did feel a wee bit left out, [so] would phone them up and start hanging about again, but see afterwards I would just be thinking, "What the fuck are you doing, man, why get into all this shit again?" That's all it is, shit ... I still get that, but a bit. I am trying though to just be done with it. Difficult, when that's all your friends do [crime].'

Consistent with other research, religiosity and spirituality can promote positive identity transformation (Flores, 2013; Deuchar, 2018). But, as Ash describes here, people often had to hit "rock bottom" first before extricating themselves from a life of crime:

'[I] would gamble the lot, plus my wage ... Was fucked up, man ... I hit rock bottom ... no home, got sacked, pure trusted no one, [and] kept having pure fucked up thoughts, man ... I had to change, but see when you try to you can't if you're still around the same people and the same situations as before ... I went from always having cash, basically free drugs, a [girlfriend], loads of mates, and always going out, to just hanging about myself and working a wee shitty job I managed to get. The money was pure pish but I needed a low income for the sake of my soul, cause I had been pure obsessed wi' money before. Was a pure humbling experience ... What I lost in material things, I was making up for inside myself.'

Concluding remarks

A key variable in the desistance process for our sample was religion and spirituality. The narratives show that Christianity was both a *method* and *motive* for desistance (see Decker et al, 2022) and these processes are not confined to North and South American experiences, where they have been observed previously (for example Brenneman, 2011; Flores, 2013). Belief in a higher power is associated with grief through ritual and process which may, as we describe in the context of desistance, manifest as an epiphany rather than a gradual movement towards self-identity transformation, or an inexplicable feeling of transcendental support replacing the grief of loss and psychic disruption of well-being. One trope of the complexity of desistance is captured through the image of 'desisted as nomad' and desistance as 'endless' (Philipps, 2017, p 92). Hallett and McCoy (2014, p 868) claim that 'pathways to desistance involve highly subjective assessments of agency and structure', thus illustrating not only its complexity, but also the individual heterogeneity of routes to desistance, which quantitative research has demonstrated is premised upon the emergence of pro-social identities (for example Rocque et al, 2016).

Of course, while this is important, it has to be noted that many of our sample who were ex-offenders were accessed through outreach groups tied to church organizations. This could well have created a sample bias. Also, given that the research sampled people involved in more serious and organized crime, they tended to be older with longer offending histories. Such individuals cannot be enticed out of crime by entry-level jobs and conventional intervention services at sports and recreation centres that cater to youth.

SEVEN

Conclusion

The aim of this book was to share insights from over a decade of empirical research in Glasgow and West Scotland, an area with a long history of gang- and drug-related crime and violence (Fraser 2015; McLean and Densley, 2020). Through qualitative interviews with (ex-)offenders and practitioners, we have been able to explore the nature of robbery within the context of the illicit drugs trade, specifically examining the way in which robbery has evolved and how, as offenders move through their criminal careers, opportunistic violent robbery is used as a means of acquiring symbolic capital before graduating to more serious and organized robbery ventures. The motivations of those involved in street robbery and the nature and patterns of robbery were also captured. We have drawn attention to why drug dealers can be easy targets for robbery, how robbery can provide offenders and victims relief from social strain, but also how robbery can lead to cycles of revenge that initiate further violent action.

Robbery has remained a comparatively under-researched crime even though it is a serious violent crime and it is a defining feature of the more deeply explored illicit drugs trade (Marsh, 2019). Our research conforms with prior studies that identified how street robbery emerges against the backdrop of unemployment, social deprivation, and drug abuse (Wright and Decker, 1997a; Contreras, 2012). However, a major contribution of this book is moving beyond any narrow focus on victim/offender typologies to consider how robbery presents differently in different social contexts. The findings point to the limits of rational choice theory as an explanation for robbery, and the need to consider the wider structural context of crime. In some social contexts, opportunistic robbery was common, particularly at the lower and more disorganized levels of the drug trade. Here, rapid risk assessments of situational factors and personal attributes of dealers were conducted. In some cases, our participants indicated that opportunistic robbery could later lead to engaging in techniques like catfishing, where victims were selected online and attacks became technologically enhanced and carefully coordinated.

However, robbery more often emerged as a by-product of serious organized crime wherein robbing drug dealers and users was a means to achieve personal expressive and instrumental goals. While some people commit robbery for material gain, others do it to sustain a hedonistic lifestyle within a street culture that prioritizes symbolic forms of criminality (Wright et al, 2006). Likewise, others simply engage in robbery for the thrill and buzz it may provide (see Katz, 1988).

From the late 1980s onwards, serious offenders capitalized on the expansion and diversification of the illegal drugs trade to become less involved in commercial robbery and more engaged in robbery as a by-product of market-based organized crime (namely drug dealing). In other words, robbery evolved from a commercial orientation to a violent street orientation linked to drug markets, confirming earlier insights by O'Mahoney and Ellis (2009). Our data suggest that the addictive attributes of drug users could result in lack of trust among users, dealers, and friends and that criminals were more likely to be motivated by easier targets (namely drug users), particularly with revolutions in security and policing meaning that bank robbery had effectively become obsolete. As such, the taking of action against dealers had become justified within the context of drug supply being viewed as a 'dirty' trade. Thus, neutralization techniques were used by our participants to justify their actions and regard their victims as vermin. At the same time, however, monetary rewards were viewed as the main motivation for street robbery among our participating (ex-)offenders and thereby a means of improving their financial position.

Implications for practice and policy

The findings show clearly that robbery, for the most part, is not random. Most victims know their attackers, some were friends or even family. While this insight is shaped by the nature of our sample (that is, the nature of snowball sampling and sampling career criminals means that networks overlap) it also reflects the reality of the crime. Robbery is driven by a small number of individuals – mostly disadvantaged young men – who share some connection to the illicit drugs trade. Drug use and supply precedes robbery for some people, but robbery precedes drug use and supply for others. The interpersonal origins of robbery can be hard to grasp from the outside, but from the inside it is well understood that robberies can escalate and turn deadly if someone pulls a weapon, or if groups competing for market share hold a grudge, or try to settle a score and use robbery as a means of retaliation.

If robbery tends to happen between people and over issues that are known to many in the wider community, efforts to reduce – or 'interrupt' – robbery that make use of trusted relationships and deep local knowledge are key (Butts et al, 2015). We need to equip individuals whose social circumstances put them at elevated risk for robbery offending and/or victimization with the skills and resources they need to avoid, de-escalate, and manage the robbery scenarios that regularly arise in their lives. These programmes sometimes operate in schools, like the Growing Against Violence project, which provides small-group counselling, skill-building, and gangs resistance education and training for youth (Densley et al, 2017). The also operate on the streets, like the Cure Violence programme, which deploys trusted messengers – often formerly incarcerated community members – to reach out to people at high risk of violence (Butts et al, 2015). In Glasgow, programmes operated under the city's Violence Reduction Unit (VRU) and Community Initiative to Reduce Violence (CIRV), provide intensive support, training, and substance abuse treatment to youths at highest risk of violence. These 'focused deterrence' programmes are associated with a significant reduction in violence city-wide (Batchelor et al, 2019; Deuchar, 2013; Williams et al, 2014).

Violence intervention is difficult work and can be executed poorly, so training and technical assistance (including for programme evaluation) are important. However, robbery prevention efforts must amount to more than just programmes. For example, we can make Glasgow and West Scotland safer just by changing the physical environment. Robberies in our study tended to occur in neglected communities and communal spaces that provided cover for both planned and spontaneous crimes, from poorly lit back alleys to underpasses and car parks. We can 'design out' these crimes by employing basic situational crime prevention measures like installing better street lighting and transforming abandoned places into neat, grass-covered areas (Lasley, 1999; Clarke, 2012). Better maintained surroundings prevent people from feeling that they can conduct criminal activity without scrutiny. While close attention to physical spaces has echoes of the controversial 'broken windows theory' (Wilson and Kelling, 1982), which in the 1980s and 1990s was used to support the massive expansion of 'stop and search' style policing in poor neighbourhoods (Deuchar et al, 2019), rehabilitating public spaces is about more than just policing.

Police do still have a role to play, indeed The Center for Problem Orientated Policing at Arizona State University (https://popcenter.asu.edu/content/problem-guides-category-0) has extensive guides on robbery mitigation strategies. Our findings hold the capacity to further inform Police Scotland (the national force for Scotland) in how best to identify the young men who are most 'at risk' for robbery offending and victimization. By focusing on the people and places where robbery converges, officers could draw upon multi-agency collaboration to initiate mentoring interventions that seek to educate young men about the impact of violence while also actively deflecting them from engaging in patterns of related online criminality such as 'catfishing', and from the allure of the drug market in general as a means of preventing their progression to young crime gangs or recruitment into organized crime (Densley et al, 2019; Harding et al, 2019).

Of course, immediate links can be drawn between the strategic planning of Police Scotland and their published reports on the four Ds – detect, divert, disrupt, and dismantle – for tackling organized criminal networks in the country (see Scottish Government, 2015; 2016). The findings here can offer up some insights into tactical and operational implications. The research first of all indicates the changing nature of robbery and how this may have shifted from places to people. This means that offenders may also be victims and vice versa and the people who have been robbed in certain instances may themselves be involved in activities which are illegal. It is crucial that criminal justice actors do not blame victims for being victimized because this will only force them to seek street justice for their affairs. Should police treat victims with contempt or suspicion it will have a lasting impact on the victim themselves in coming forward in the future, and also begin to undermine public confidence in police more generally. This was clear in Chapter One from the interaction between Ricky and the officers who attended the robbery scene immediately after Ricky had been attacked – he was assumed to be a potential drug dealer or user.

It would seem that in relation to 'divert', situational crime prevention efforts may have inadvertently displaced the crime of commerical robbery, encouraging career criminals to divert their attentions to robbery in the sphere of illegality, which, in turn, helps them avoid police detection and stay under the radar. This of course brings its own issues with regard to trying to police such an arena. This brings us to the goals of disrupt and dismantle. Any robbery that occurs in the context of the illegal drugs trade is a by-product of the existence of the drugs trade itself: essentially it is a criminal act (robbery) nested within a pre-existing criminal act (drug dealing). Thus, robbery is carried out in such a context precisely because it lies outside the realm of police intervention. While police are undertaking extensive efforts through dedicated crime units to tackling (organized) drug crime and its related harms, namely the systemic violence of the market (Findley, 2012), it is ultimately a losing battle when drugs are treated as a police matter alone. In the end, drug use is a societal issue, with the implication being that Glasgow and West Scotland must continue to invest in violence prevention as part of a broader public health infrastructure that is equipped to reach people where they are at. Police and violence prevention programmes alone cannot solve the social ailments that give rise to crimes of desperation. Only thriving communities with well-functioning public services, strong schools, and economic opportunity can do that.

Glasgow and West Scotland's illicit drugs trade has grown for a number of reasons, including but not exhausted by: global capitalism, deindustrialization, the failure to replace heavy industry with other types of masculine employment, the consumer society and continued promotion of hedonistic lifestyles (see Densley et al, 2018; Irwin-Rogers, 2019; McPhee et al, 2019). Drug dealing is a dangerous game, even though in recent years it has become more open and accessible to those actors who in prior years would not have become dealers. As such, many see it as a business in which profits and potential fortunes can be made, but also where amateur drug dealers are easy pickings. While some people 'bump' others, run up debts and fail to pay, or commit theft to avoid paying for drugs, violent robbery is another solution, at times contingent on the convergence of motivated offenders, suitable targets, and an absence of capable guardianship (Cohen and Felson, 1979).

Further, our data suggest that drug addiction was at times the main contributing factor to robbery offending and victimization (echoing earlier insights by Casey et al, 2009; Jacobs,

2000; Harding et al, 2019). Drug use influenced the frequency, duration, latency, and intensity of robbery careers, as we saw from a number of case studies in this book. Robbery within illicit drug markets will continue to exist as long as illicit drug markets exist. We cannot eliminate the problem of robbery in this context, and its related harms, without addressing the wider issue of drugs and, relatedly, organized crime (Fraser et al, 2018).

Most robberies in this study took place within the retail-level and lower end of the drugs trade. This is largely because those who operate in such arenas may not have the capability or networks themselves to draw upon others to defend themselves against opportunistic violent attackers. Similarly, the transactions which take place in such arenas are often more public, more open, and more regular; as well as being for smaller cash-in-hand profits. Additionally, dealers are often dealing with those who may actually be intoxicated at the time of transaction. As such, they are more inclined to act irrationally or spontaneously. Thus, the very thing which creates the contact initially is the context in which robbery can occur.

At the higher echelons of the drugs trade, cash transactions become fewer and deals involve better established relationships. However, this only recalibrates the risk-reward calculus – it doesn't mitigate it entirely. Robbery offenders and victims tend to be young people and Generation Z's primary source of communication, Snapchat, which uses end-to-end encryption on photos shared between its users and is built to immediately delete messages, has been appropriated to become a bulletin board for illegal goods and services (for example Storrod and Densley, 2017). Previous studies (see Demant et al, 2019), including our own prior work on illegal drugs markets (for example Densley et al, 2018; McLean, 2019; McPhee et al, 2019), indicate that while online deals still represent a small portion of the overall drugs trade, dealers and users are increasingly finding each other over the internet. Online direct-to-consumer advertising comes with new robbery risks. We see from the case study of Gee that even platforms such as Gumtree can be exploited to entrap victims for robbery. Be safe online is one recommendation that comes from this, but social media platforms must simultaneously do more to protect their users from robbery victimization, such as by verifying who is posting content online and better moderating what they are posting.

A further implication from the research is that robbery associated with the illicit drugs trade often is weapon-enabled. At the time of writing, the United States is experiencing a surge in gun violence, including robbery with firearms. It may seem odd to suggest that a book with so many examples of *knife* robbery has much to teach American criminology about robbery in general, but armed robbery in all forms involves some close proximity of robber and victim. The robber must be close enough to the victim, even when armed, to make the threat of the weapon credible. And while knives were common in Glasgow and can be purchased widely, the most dangerous robberies were committed using firearms. In simple assaults, knives may do the trick, but in robbery, which is largely about 'creating the illusion of impending death' (Wright and Decker, 1997b), firearms were preferred even if only for display in the case of replica models.

Gun laws in the UK are among the toughest in the world (Squires, 2014). Very few people, even police officers, carry firearms. All handguns and modern semi-automatic rifles, the type of guns that can be fired rapidly without needing to be reloaded, are banned. And yet, a majority of the robbers who acted with intent in our study claimed access to guns and a minority of them had used guns in the commission of a crime. Sporting rifles and shotguns were common. If you legally own a firearm, therefore, it is important you keep it locked and hidden when not being used and you remain cautious about who knows you own it. Illegal firearms like sawed-off-shotguns, Browning pistols, even Glock handguns obtained through criminal networks and armourers in Europe, also were mentioned. The implication here is that more can be done beyond existing gun laws to limit, or better track, the transfer of firearms, including antique and deactivated weapons. Regulation of firearm ammunition also is important because prior research (for example McLean and Densley, 2020) has shown that offenders will choose knives over guns if the availability of bullets and shells renders guns unreliable, unpredictable, even inoperable.

We recognize that our research had its limitations, in so much that it was confined to one geographical area of Scotland, our methodological approach was focused solely on the use of semi-structured interviews with a sample which was almost exclusively male (ex-)offenders. As such, we need to be cautious about generalizing the findings to other parts of the UK, or even Scotland. However, we believe that the insights we have gained draw attention to the nuanced nature of street offending and robbery within the context of illicit drug markets, gangs and organized crime. This book is one of only a handful of its kind, thus while limited in scope, by focusing on robbery within Scotland's illegal drugs trade, it makes an important contribution to knowledge. Future research needs to explore the wider practice of robbery in other contexts, and similarly examine how and why patterns of robbery change and evolve in time and space and as offenders progress through gang hierarchies. The role of young women within organized crime and their potential relationship with the coordination of street robbery within the context of drug distribution networks should also be explored. It is hoped that this book may help to stimulate such research.

Notes

one   On Robbery

[1]   The profanity and potentially offensive language used in this book comes directly from our research subjects and reflects the verbatim nature of the interview data. We are committed to preserving the spoken word as is.

[2]   In Scotland, scheme is an informal name for a public housing complex.

four   Robbery in Action

[1]   A busy open market characterized by stalls and street sellers at the edge of Glasgow city centre.

[2]   When referring to criminal 'crews', Glaswegians often replace the c with the letter k.

References

Anderson, E. (1999) *Code of the street.* Norton.

Batchelor, S., Armstrong, S. and MacLellan, D. (2019) *Taking stock of violence in Scotland.* The Scottish Centre for Crime and Justice Research.

Black, W. (2014) *The best way to rob a bank is to own one.* University of Texas Press.

Bolden, C. (2020) *Out of the red.* Rutgers University Press.

Boyle, J. (1977) *A sense of freedom.* Pan Books.

Brenneman, R. (2011) *Homies and hermanos.* Oxford University Press.

Butts, J., Roman, C., Bostwick, L. and Porter, J. (2015) Cure violence: a public health model to reduce gun violence. *Annual Review of Public Health*, 36(1), 39–53.

Carlsson, C. (2012) Using 'turning points' to understand processes of change in offending: notes from a Swedish study on life courses and crime. *The British Journal of Criminology*, 52(1), 1–16.

Casey, J., Hay, G., Godfrey, C. and Parrot, S. (2009) *Assessing the scale and impact of illicit drug markets in Scotland.* Scottish Government.

Clarke, R.V. (2012) Opportunity makes the thief. Really? And so what? *Crime Science*, 1, 3.

Cohen, L. and Felson, M. (1979) Social change and crime rate trends: a routine activity approach. *American Sociological Review*, 44(4), 588–608.

Contreras, R. (2012) *The stickup kids.* University of California Press.

Coomber, R. (2006) *Pusher myths.* Free Association Books.

Coomber, R. and Moyle, L. (2014) Beyond drug dealing: developing and extending the concept of 'social supply' of illicit drugs to 'minimally commercial supply'. *Drugs: Education, Prevention and Policy*, 21(2), 157–64.

Cornish, D. and Clarke, R. (1986) *The reasoning criminal.* Springer.

Daly, M. (2017) What happened to the 'Trainspotting' generation of heroin users? *Vice*. Retrieved from: www.vice.com/en_us/article/8qqa94/this-is-what-happened-to-the-trainspotting-generation-of-heroin-users

Davies, A. (2013) *City of gangs*. Hodder & Stoughton.

Deakin, J., Smithson, H., Spencer, J. and Medina-Ariza, J. (2007) Taxing on the streets: understanding the methods and process of street robbery. *Crime Prevention and Community Safety*, 9, 52–67.

Decker, S.H. (1996) Collective and normative features of gang violence. *Justice Quarterly*, 13(2), 243–64.

Decker, S.H. and Curry, G.D. (2002) Gangs, gang homicide, and gang loyalty: organized crime and disorganized criminals. *Journal of Criminal Justice*, 30(4), 343–52.

Decker, S.H. and Van Winkle, B. (1994) Slinging dope: the role of gangs and gang members in drug sales. *Justice Quarterly*, 11(4), 583–604.

Decker, S.H. and Van Winkle, B. (1996) *Life in the gang*. Cambridge University Press.

Decker, S.H., Pyrooz, D. and Densley, J. (2022) *On gangs*. Temple University Press.

Demant, J., Bakken, S.A., Oksanen, A. and Gunnlaugsson, H. (2019) Drug dealing on Facebook, Snapchat and Instagram: a qualitative analysis of novel drug markets in the Nordic countries. *Drug and Alcohol Review*, 38(4), 377–85.

Densley, J. (2012) Street gang recruitment: signaling, screening, and selection. *Social Problems*, 59(3), 301–21.

Densley, J. (2013) *How gangs work*. Palgrave Macmillan.

Densley, J. (2014) It's gang life, but not as we know it: the evolution of gang business. *Crime & Delinquency*, 60(4), 517–46.

Densley, J. (2018) Gang joining. In: H. Pontell (ed) *Oxford research encyclopedia of criminology and criminal justice*, Oxford University Press.

Densley, J. and Pyrooz, D. (2019) A signaling perspective on disengagement from gangs. *Justice Quarterly*, 36(1), 31–58.

Densley, J., Adler, J., Zhu, L. and Lambine, M. (2017) Growing against gangs and violence: findings from a process and outcome evaluation. *Psychology of Violence*, 7(2), 242–52.

Densley, J., McLean, R., Deuchar, R. and Harding, S. (2018) An altered state? Emergent changes to illicit drug markets and distribution networks in Scotland. *International Journal of Drug Policy*, 58, 113–20.

Densley, J., McLean, R., Deuchar, R. and Harding, S. (2019) Progression from cafeteria to à la carte offending: Scottish organised crime narratives. *Howard Journal of Crime and Justice*, 58(2), 161–79.

Deuchar, R. (2009) *Gangs, marginalised youth and social capital*. Trentham.

Deuchar R. (2013) *Policing youth violence: transatlantic connections*. IOE Press.

Deuchar, R. (2018) *Gangs and spirituality*. Palgrave Macmillan.

Deuchar, R., McLean, R. and Holligan, C. (2022) *Gangs, drugs and youth adversity*. Bristol University Press.

Deuchar, R., Miller, J. and Densley, J. (2019) The lived experience of stop and search in Scotland: there are two sides to every story. *Police Quarterly*, 22(4), 416–51.

Elder, G. (1994) Time, human agency, and social change: perspectives on the life course. *Social Psychology Quarterly*, 57 (1), 4–15.

Ezell, M. and Cohen, L. (2005) *Desisting from crime*. Oxford University Press.

Feeney, F. (1986) Robbers as decision-makers. In: D.B. Cornish and R. Clarke (eds) *The Reasoning Criminal*, Springer, pp 1–16.

Felson, M. and Clarke. R.V. (1998) *Opportunity makes the thief: practical theory for crime prevention*. Police Research Series, Paper 98. Home Office.

Ferris, P. (2005) *Vendetta*. Black and White Publishing.

Findlay, R. (2012) *Caught in the crossfire: Scotland's deadliest drugs war*. Barlinn Limited.

Flores, E.O. (2013) *God's gangs*. NYU Press.

Fraser. A. (2015) *Urban legends*. Oxford University Press.

Fraser, A., Hamilton-Smith, N., Clark, A., Atkinson, C., Graham, W., McBride, M., Doyle, M. and Hobbs, D. (2018) *Community experiences of serious organised crime in Scotland.* Scottish Government.

Gambetta, D. (1993) *The Sicilian Mafia.* Harvard University Press.

Gambetta, D. (2009) *Codes of the underworld.* Princeton University Press.

Glasgow Indicators Project (2015) *Overview poverty.* Glasgow Centre for Population Health.

Goldstein, P.J. (1985) The drugs/violence nexus: a tripartite conceptual framework. *Journal of Drug Issues,* 15, 493–506.

Gottfredson, M. and Hirschi, T. (1990) *A general theory of crime.* Stanford University Press.

Gundur, R.V. (2019) Settings matter: examining Protection's influence on the illicit drug trade in convergence settings in the Paso del Norte metropolitan area. *Crime Law & Social Change,* 72, 339–60.

Gundur, R.V. (2020) Finding the sweet spot: optimizing criminal careers within the context of illicit enterprise. *Deviant Behavior,* 41(3), 378–97.

Hall, S., Critcher, C., Jefferson, T., Clarke, J. and Roberts, B. (1978) *Policing the crisis.* Macmillan.

Hallett, M. and McCoy, J. (2014) Religiously motivated desistance: an exploratory study. *International Journal of Offender Therapy and Comparative Criminology,* 59(8), 855–72.

Hallsworth, S. (2005) *Street crime.* Willan.

Hallsworth, S. (2013) *The gang and beyond.* Palgrave Macmillan.

Harding, S. (2014) *The street casino.* Policy Press.

Harding, S., Deuchar, R., Densley, J. and McLean, R. (2019) A typology of street robbery and gang organization: insights from qualitative research in Scotland. *The British Journal of Criminology,* 59(4), 879–97.

Hart, C. (2021) *Drug use for grown-ups.* Penguin.

Hobbs, D. (1988) *Doing the business.* Clarendon Press.

Hobbs, D. (1995) *Bad business.* Oxford University Press.

Holligan, C., McLean, R. and Deuchar, R. (2017) Weapon-carrying among young men in Glasgow: street scripts and signals in uncertain social spaces. *Critical Criminology,* 25(1), 137–51.

Howell, J.C. and Decker, S.H. (1999) *The youth gangs, drugs, and violence connection*. US Department of Justice, Office of Justice Programs, Office of Juvenile Justice and Delinquency Prevention.

Hutton, F. (2005) Risky business: gender, drug dealing, and risk. *Addiction Research and Theory*, 13(6), 545–54.

Irwin-Rogers, K. (2019) Illicit drug markets, consumer capitalism and the rise of social media: a toxic trap for young people. *Critical Criminology*, 27(4), 591–610.

Jacobs, B. (2000) *Robbing drug dealers*. Aldine de Gruyter.

Jacobs, B. and Wright, R. (1999) Stick up, street culture, and offender motivation. *Criminology*, 37(1), 149–74.

Jacobs, B. and Wright, R. (2006) *Street justice*. Cambridge University Press.

Jacobs, B. and Wright, R. (2008) Moralistic street robbery. *Crime & Delinquency*, 54(4), 511–31.

Johnson, A. and Densley, J. (2018) Rio's new social order: how religion signals disengagement from prison gangs. *Qualitative Sociology*, 41(2), 243–62.

Johnson, G. (2017) *The devil: Britain's most feared underworld taxman*. Mainstream.

Katz, J. (1988) *Seductions of crime*. Basic Books.

Lasley, J. (1999) 'Designing out' gang homicides and street assaults: research in brief. National Institute of Justice.

Laub, J.H. and Sampson, R.J. (1993) Turning points in the life course: why change matters to the study of crime. *Criminology*, 31(3), 301–25.

Lauger, T. (2014) Violent stories: personal narratives, street socialization, and the negotiation of street culture among street-oriented youth. *Criminal Justice Review*, 39(2), 182–200.

Mamayek, C., Paternoster, R. and Loughran, T.A. (2016) Self-control as self-regulation: a return to control theory. *Deviant Behavior*, 38(8), 1–22.

Marsh, B. (2019) *The logic of violence*. Routledge.

Maruna, S. (2001) *Making good*. American Psychological Association.

McAdams, D.P. (1997) *The stories we live by*. Guilford Press.

McCarron, M. (2014) It is in the interests of justice and health to decriminalise drug users. *Scottish Justice Matters*, 2, 17–18.

McCarthy, B. and Hagan, J. (1995) Getting into street crime: the structure and process of criminal embeddedness. *Social Science Research*, 24(1), 63–95.

McCarthy, B. and Hagan, J. (2001) When crime pays: capital, competence, and criminal success. *Social Forces*, 79(3), 1035–59.

McDiarmid, C. (2018) *Scottish criminal law essentials* (3rd ed). Edinburgh University Press.

McLean, R. (2018) An evolving gang model in contemporary Scotland. *Deviant Behavior*, 39, 309–21.

McLean, R. (2019) *Gangs, drugs, and (dis)organised crime*. Bristol University Press.

McLean, R. and Densley, J. (2020) *Scotland's gang members: life and crime in Glasgow*. Palgrave Macmillan.

McLean, R., Densley, J. and Deuchar, R. (2018) Situating gangs within Scotland's illegal drugs market(s). *Trends in Organized Crime*, 21, 147–71.

McLean, R., Robinson, G. and Densley, J. (2020) *County lines: criminal networks and evolving drug markets in Britain*. Springer.

McPhee, I., Holligan, C., McLean, R. and Deuchar, R. (2019) Dr. Jekyll and Mr. Hyde: the strange case of the two selves of clandestine drug users. *Drugs and Alcohol Today*, 19(2), 133–46.

O'Mahoney, B. and Ellis, S. (2009) *Essex boy*. Mainstream.

Parker, H., Aldridge, J. and Measham, F. (1998) *Illegal leisure: the normalisation of adolescent drug use*. Routledge.

Pearson, G. and Hobbs, D. (2001) *Middle market drug distribution*. Home Office.

Philipps, J. (2017). Towards a rhizomatic understanding of the desistance journey. *The Howard Journal*, 56, 92–104.

Pickering, J., Kintrea, K. and Bannister, J. (2012) Invisible walls and visible youth: territoriality among young people in British cities. *Urban Studies*, 49(5), 945–60.

Pitts, J. (2008) *Reluctant gangsters*. Willan.

Presser, L. and Sandberg, S. (eds) (2015) *Narrative criminology*. NYU Press.

Rahman, M., McLean, R., Deuchar, R. and Densley, J. (2020) Who are the enforcers? The motives and methods of muscle for hire in West Scotland and the West Midlands. *Trends in Organized Crime*, doi: 10.1007/s12117-020-09382-y

Reuter, P. (1983). *Disorganized crime*. The MIT Press.

Rocque, M., Chad, P. and Paternoster, R. (2016) Identities through time: an exploration of identity change as a cause of desistance. *Justice Quarterly*, 33(1), 45–72.

Roks, R., Leukfeldt, E.R. and Densley, J. (2020) The hybridization of street offending in the Netherlands. *British Journal of Criminology*, 61(4), 926–45.

Rosenfeld, R., Jacobs, B. and Wright, R. (2003) Snitching and the code of the streets. *British Journal of Criminology*, 43, 291–309.

Scottish Government (2015) Scotland's serious organised crime strategy: annual report.

Scottish Government (2016) Scotland's serious organised crime strategy: annual report.

Scottish Government (2020) Scottish index of multiple deprivation. Retrieved from: www.gov.scot/collections/scottish-index-of-multiple-deprivation-2020/

Short, J.F. Jr. and Strodtbeck, F.L. (1965) *Group process and gang delinquency*. University of Chicago Press.

Shover, N. (1996) *Great pretenders*. Westview.

Smith, J. (2003) *The nature of personal robbery*. Home Office.

Squires, P. (2014) *Gun crime in global contexts*. Routledge.

Stockdale, J. and Gresham, P. (1998) *Tackling street robbery: a comparative evaluation of operation eagle eye*. Home Office.

Storrod, M.L. and Densley, J. (2017) 'Going viral' and 'Going country': the expressive and instrumental activities of street gangs on social media. *Journal of Youth Studies*, 20(6), 677–96.

Sykes, G. and Matza, D. (1957) Techniques of neutralization: a theory of delinquency. *American Sociological Review*, 22, 664–70.

Tilley, N., Smith, J., Finer, S., Erol, R., Charles, C. and Dobby, J. (2004) *Problem-solving street crime: practical lessons from the street crime initiative*. Home Office.

Topalli, V., Fornango, R. and Wright, R. (2002) Drug dealers, robbery, and retaliation: vulnerability, deterrence, and the contagion of violence. *British Journal of Criminology*, 42(2), 337–51.

Turanovic, J. and Pratt, T. (2019) *Thinking about victimization*. Routledge.

Veysey, B., Martinez, D. and Christian, J. (2013) 'Getting out': a summary of qualitative research on desistance across the life course. In: C. Gibson and M. Krohn (eds) *Handbook of life course criminology: emerging trends for future research*, Springer, pp 233–60.

von Lampe, K. (2016) *Organized crime*. Sage.

Walsh, D., McCartney, G., Collins, C., Taulbut, M. and Batty, G.D. (2017) History, politics and vulnerability: explaining excess mortality in Scotland and Glasgow. *Public Health*, 151, 1–12.

Walters, G. (1990) *The criminal lifestyle*. Sage.

Whittaker, A., Densley, J., Cheston, L., Tyrell, T., Higgins, M., Felix-Baptiste, C. and Havard, T. (2020) Reluctant gangsters revisited: the evolution of gangs from postcodes to profits. *European Journal on Criminal Policy and Research*, 26(1), 1–22.

Williams, D.J., Currie, D., Linden, W. and Donelly, P. (2014) Addressing gang-related violence in Glasgow: a preliminary pragmatic quasi-experimental evaluation of the Community Initiative to Reduce Violence (CIRV). *Aggression and Violent Behavior*, 19(6), 686–91.

Wilson, J. and Kelling, G. (1982) Broken windows: police and neighborhood safety. *Atlantic Monthly*, 249, 29–38.

Windle, J. (2013) Tuckers firm: a case study of British organised crime. *Trends in Organized Crime*, 16(4), 382–96.

Windle, J. and Briggs, D. (2015) Going solo: the social organisation of drug dealing within a London street gang. *Journal of Youth Studies*, 18(9), 1170–85.

Winlow, S. (2001) *Badfellas*. Berg.

Wright, R. and Bennett, T. (1990) Exploring the offender's perspective: observing and interviewing criminals. In: K. Kempf (ed.) *Measurement issues in criminology*, Springer-Verlag, pp 138–51.

Wright, R. and Decker, S.H. (1997a) *Armed robbers in action*. Northeastern University Press.

Wright, R. and Decker, S.H. (1997b) Creating the illusion of impending death: armed robbers in action. *Harry Frank Guggenheim Review*, 2, 10–18.

Wright, R., Brookman, F. and Bennett, T. (2006) The foreground dynamics of street robbery in Britain. *British Journal of Criminology*, 46(1), 1–15.

Zimring, F. and Hawkins, G. (1999) *Crime is not the problem*. Oxford University Press.

Index